LOUISIANA SUGAR PLANTATIONS DURING THE CIVIL WAR

CHARLES P. ROLAND

LOUISIANA
SUGAR PLANTATIONS
DURING THE CIVIL WAR

With a New Foreword by
JOHN DAVID SMITH

LOUISIANA STATE UNIVERSITY PRESS
BATON ROUGE AND LONDON

Copyright © 1957 by E. J. Brill, Leiden, Netherlands
New material copyright © 1997 by Louisiana State University Press
LSU Press edition published by arrangement with the author
All rights reserved
Manufactured in the United States of America

Louisiana Paperback Edition, 1997
06 05 04 03 02 01 00 99 98 97   5 4 3 2 1

Library of Congress Cataloging-in-Publication Data

Roland, Charles Pierce, 1918–
   Louisiana sugar plantations during the Civil War / Charles P.
Roland ; with a new foreword by John David Smith. —Louisiana pbk.
ed.
    p.   cm.
   Originally published: Leiden : E. J. Brill, 1957.
   Includes bibliographical references (p.   ) and index.
   ISBN 0-8071-2221-1 (paper : alk. paper)
   1. Louisiana—History—Civil War, 1861–1865. 2. Sugar growing—
Louisiana. 3. Plantation life—Louisiana. I. Title.
E565.R62   1997
976.3'05—dc21   97-24368
                                                                                      CIP

The paper in this book meets the guidelines for permanence and durability of the
Committee on Production Guidelines for Book Longevity of the Council on Library
Resources. ∞

To
ALLIE LEE ROLAND
In appreciation for unflagging encouragement and support

CONTENTS

Acknowledgments ix
Foreword xi

I The Cane Country 1
II The Peculiar Institution and Plantation Routine 10
III Secession and Faraway War 19
IV Eve of Invasion 27
V Blockade and Invasion 42
VI Winds of Destruction 57
VII Barren Harvest 75
VIII Emancipated Labor 92
IX From Exultation to Despair 117
X Frolics and Frivolities 129
XI Epilogue 137

Bibliography 140
Index 144

ACKNOWLEDGMENTS

The author wishes to express appreciation to the many individuals and institutions whose support and assistance have made possible the publication of this book. He is especially indebted to Professor Francis Butler Simkins, who gave unsparingly of his time and knowledge in reading the original manuscript and offering advice for its improvement. Professor Bell I. Wiley likewise gave assistance in the early stages of the author's research and later read the completed manuscript and made many excellent suggestions for its revision. Professor William R. Hogan extended to the author both encouragement and sound editorial recommendations. Various members of the Department of History, Louisiana State University, provided constructive criticism of the manuscript in an early form. The staff of the Department of Archives, Louisiana State University, gave invaluable assistance in making available many of the materials from which this study has grown. Professor Barnes F. Lathrop placed at the writer's disposal his extensive unpublished study on the Pugh sugar plantations and life in lower Louisiana during the Civil War. Finally, the author gratefully acknowledges the generous financial support rendered by the Research Council, Tulane University, that has led to the revision of the manuscript and publication of this volume.

FOREWORD

Forty years ago, during the initial phases of the civil rights revolution and on the eve of the Civil War centennial, Charles P. Roland published *Louisiana Sugar Plantations During the Civil War* (1957), the first monograph to examine the wartime metamorphosis of Louisiana's sugar agriculture.[1] Though J. Carlyle Sitterson published his economic history *Sugar Country: The Cane Sugar Industry in the South, 1753–1950* in 1954, and Kenneth M. Stampp published his classic *The Peculiar Institution: Slavery in the Ante-Bellum South* in 1956, the 1950s was a period of flux for works on slavery and emancipation. During this decade, according to historian Joe Gray Taylor, "no publisher was interested in a manuscript dealing with [Louisiana] slavery, and it took the civil rights movement to arouse interest."[2]

Roland's pioneering work, published by E. J. Brill in the Netherlands, focuses on the transition—for cane-county folk, white and black—that occurred as Union troops penetrated Louisiana's sugar districts during the Civil War. In detailing this transition, the author examines closely the impact of secession, war, and Federal occupation on the state's sugar parishes, especially the plantation routine and the *Zeitgeist* of those white Louisianans in the throes of defeat and military rule. Roland's slender first book contains those qualities that characterize his many later studies: elegant prose, dry wit, and careful research.[3] While he bases his analysis of the rise and fall of Louisiana's wartime sugar industry largely on unpublished plantation diaries, journals, and correspondence, Roland also consulted newspapers, official documents, regimental histories, and annual sugar reports. In addition, he pored over published diaries, letters, and reminiscences of persons who lived in or visited the sugar

---

1. Roland's book originated as a master's thesis supervised by Professor Bell I. Wiley at Louisiana State University in 1948 and was expanded into a doctoral dissertation, supervised by Professor Francis Butler Simkins, three years later. Roland published some of the fruits of his early research in "Difficulties of Civil War Sugar Planting in Louisiana," *Louisiana Historical Quarterly*, XXXVIII (1955), 40–62.

2. Joe Gray Taylor, "A New Look at Slavery in Louisiana," in *Louisiana's Black Heritage*, ed. Robert R. Macdonald, John R. Kemp, and Edward F. Haas (New Orleans, 1979), 190.

3. For a selected bibliography of Roland's publications, see John David Smith and Thomas H. Appleton, Jr., eds., *A Mythic Land Apart: Reassessing Southerners and Their History* (Westport, Conn., 1997), 191–95.

country during the war.

Roland portrays Louisiana's sugar land, fed by the region's many bayous and rivers, as a unique corner of the Old South. Cane plantations dominated the economy and culture of twenty-four of the state's forty-six parishes before the Civil War. Roland describes the cane country as

> a labyrinthine river land of ample cane plantations interspersed with narrow sugar farms, of white-columned mansions contrasting with humble dwellings, of tall-chimneyed sugarhouses in juxtaposition with primitive mule-drawn cane mills, of Anglo-American planters among Creole proprietors, of Irish and "Cajun" laborers in the midst of a multitude of Negro slaves, and of affluent and graceful living in the presence of rural simplicity and back-breaking toil.

The value of Louisiana's sugar facilities was $194,000,000 in 1861. In that year sugar proprietors owned 1,291 plantations and produced 459,410 hogsheads of sugar. The 1861–1862 crop reaped the greatest harvest in the state's history.

Cane plantations—remote and self-sufficient—were atypical plantation economies, assuming multiple market and social functions. They were agricultural units where slave laborers cultivated, cut, and hauled raw sugarcane. They were also factories where slaves milled raw cane into sugar. The production process—including cultivating the crop, draining and maintaining ditches, grinding and boiling the cane, and crystallizing sugar—required more capital and more industrial skill than cotton planting. Because of its costly infrastructure, Louisiana's antebellum sugar industry depended on federal protective tariffs to flourish. Sugar entrepreneurs were among the largest slaveholders in the South and among its wealthiest citizens. They were also, Roland explains, "men of sound wit who tempered their lives with vigorous play, set the pace for the area in which they lived, and made the plantation ideal supreme."

The cane country was home to almost 140,000 black slaves as well, men and women who labored to amass the planters' fortunes. Whereas whites managed and marketed the crop, blacks worked painstakingly in the canefields, maintaining the drainage systems as well as cutting, chopping, and hauling both sugarcane and the large amounts of wood needed to fuel the furnaces for the milling process. Louisiana's sugar land was thus a society based on planter control, minimal governmental interference, and the tenets of white racial supremacy.

The Civil War overhauled lower Louisiana's sugar culture dramatically. After the fall of New Orleans on May 1, 1862, the Union army and northern agents gradually infiltrated the sugar parishes. According to Roland, for the

Yankees, Louisiana's sugar country "was a prize more precious than rubies." While some cane growers fled with their possessions—including slaves—to Texas, others tried in vain to raise their crop as before. Few succeeded. Federal troops confiscated much of the sugar planters' property. Their slaves fled in search of new lives as freedmen and freedwomen. Guerrillas and deserters from both sides preyed upon the planter elite. Dikes and canefields were laid to waste, costly boiling machinery was destroyed, sugarhouses were burned, and livestock seized. Turmoil reigned in lower Louisiana. In Roland's opinion, the wartime demise of Louisiana's cane culture was an "immense tragedy . . . the destruction of a graceful civilization."

Roland reveals how the sugar barons, who once had wielded power in Louisiana and throughout the South, stood at the mercy of the occupying army and U.S. Treasury Department officials. Many planters lost their land to bankruptcy and were forced to halt their operations. Some sold or leased their plantations to northern entrepreneurs and investors. Those in Union-occupied parishes who adjusted to the new order of things collaborated with the once-hated Yankees, resurrecting canefields, rebuilding the old sugarhouses, and putting the freedpeople to work. Planters hired the former slaves for wages on annual contracts. Blacks, determined to be free in deed as well as in word, but denied land and mules, had few options but to labor for their "new masters."[4]

Though Louisiana's sugar industry ultimately survived emancipation and Confederate defeat, Roland points out that it never fully recovered from the devastation of the war. The number of the state's sugar plantations, for example, decreased from 1,291 in 1861 to fewer than 200 in 1865. Sugar production plummeted from 459,410 hogsheads in 1861–1862 to 76,801 in 1863–1864, and to around 10,000 in 1864–1865. By the end of the conflict, the cane parishes produced less than 3 percent of the prewar crop. In terms of capital, the value of the region's sugar industry fell from $194,000,000 in 1861 to between $25,000,000 and $30,000,000 in 1865. Adapting, then, to the new way of life was painful for both races. Not until the 1890s would Louisiana sugar production equal its 1862 output. Whereas the state had close to 1,300 sugarhouses in 1860, the number had declined to only 60 by the 1950s.[5]

According to his contemporaries, Roland captured the flavor of defeat, desolation, and emancipation in Louisiana better than previous historians. Vander-

---

4. On this transformation, see Lawrence N. Powell, *New Masters: Northern Planters during the Civil War and Reconstruction* (New Haven, 1980).

5. Post–Civil War units, however, were much larger than their Old South predecessors. See John Alfred Heitmann, *The Modernization of the Louisiana Sugar Industry, 1860–1910* (Baton Rouge, 1987). For a recent overview of Louisiana's sugar industry, see Glenn R. Conrad and Ray F. Lucas, *White Gold: A Brief History of the Louisiana Sugar Industry, 1795–1995* (Lafayette, La., 1995).

bilt University's Herbert Weaver described Roland's book as "a valuable addition to the historiography of the Civil War." Raleigh Suarez praised it for chronicling "not only an industry, but also a way of life." And Charles L. Dufour of the New Orleans *Times-Picayune* concluded that Roland's study "belongs on the bookshelf of any War Between the States enthusiast or collector of Louisiana items." Others, including David Donald and May S. Ringold, identified *Louisiana Sugar Plantations* as a pioneering work on southern agriculture during the Civil War, a prototype for similar studies for other southern states. Because of its readability and its graceful prose, Roland's book received the Louisiana Library Association's Literary Award for 1957. It was commended for doing "more to preserve Louisiana's heritage than any other book published during 1957."[6]

Though frequently cited by scholars today, *Louisiana Sugar Plantations During the Civil War* differs in approach and emphasis from modern emancipation studies. Like others of his day, Roland generally viewed the emancipation experience through the eyes of the planters and blamed the dramatic postwar drop in sugar production largely on "the inefficiencies of free Negro labor in its trial stage." To a certain extent, Roland was correct, especially if one assumes that "productivity" (output per labor-hour) declined after emancipation because free labor could not be forced as readily as slave labor.

In contrast to Roland's approach in the 1950s, scholars now take much greater heed of the perspective of those enslaved, view emancipation as "process," and write of the good that came from slavery's demise. They explore the various modes of resistance by the slaves, find many explanations for the slow rebuilding of the South's postwar economy, and recount the aspirations of the freedmen and freedwomen.[7] In 1976, for example, historian C. Peter Ripley faulted Roland, along with Sitterson and Taylor, for relying too heavily on white sources and, as a result, undervaluing the efficiency of free black labor. According to Ripley, these scholars "describe events from the planters' side of the veranda. They tell the story from the particular perspective of the slave-

6. Herbert Weaver, review in *Mississippi Valley Historical Review*, XLIV (1957–1958), 559; Raleigh A. Suarez, review in *Louisiana History*, I (1960), 88; Charles L. "Pie" Dufour, "Plantations and the War," New Orleans *Times-Picayune*, March 23, 1958; James G. Randall and David Donald, *The Civil War and Reconstruction* (Boston, 1961), 760; May S. Ringold, "The Confederacy—Economic and Social Studies," in *Civil War Books: A Critical Bibliography*, ed. Allan Nevins, James I. Robertson, and Bell I. Wiley (2 vols.; Baton Rouge, 1969), II, 201; T. N. McMullan to Charles P. Roland, March 7, 1958, copy in possession of the author; "Louisiana Library Assn. Presents Annual Awards," Shreveport *Journal*, March 21, 1958.

7. See, for example, Eric Foner, *Reconstruction: America's Unfinished Revolution, 1863–1877* (New York, 1988). On the viewpoint and methodology of the new emancipation scholarship, see John David Smith, "'The World at First Neither Saw nor Understood': Documenting the Emancipation Experience," *North Carolina Historical Review*, LXXI (1994), 472–77.

holders who during the occupation period saw their way of life disappearing."[8]

Roland, however, was quite aware of the hardships endured by slaves and freedpeople. He notes, for example, "the savagery to which Negroes sometimes were subjected at the sadistic whim of the whites" and describes the abolition efforts of a freedwoman, Kitty Johnson, who led a "Civil War sit-down movement." Roland also faults white planters, whose "*a priori* condemnation" of free black labor served "to blind them to the possibility of any good in the new order, just as Federal authorities were led by their preconceptions vastly to exaggerate its immediate virtues." Like modern scholars, Roland too understood the slaves' "latent urge to escape" and commented ironically that wartime sexual unions between white Federal soldiers and blacks "should have come as no surprise to many of the planters."

Regarding the comparative economics of slave and free labor, Roland has stood firm in his belief in the relative inefficiency of free black labor during the first throes of emancipation. Critiquing Ripley's work in 1978, Roland found it "difficult to believe . . . that the freedmen were able to overcome the severities and limitations of slavery, enjoy the jubilee of emancipation, and swallow the bitter dose of being herded back on the plantation almost as if they were still in bondage, yet remain model workers through it all."[9] That is not to say, however, that Roland does not recognize the paucity of black sources as a problem, one that has plagued others of his generation of scholars as well.

Cognizant of this weakness in his book, Roland explained recently that he considered "the most glaring gap" in his sources to be "that of the unavailability of contemporary slave accounts, a deficiency that robs the book of an adequate description of [slaves'] feelings and motivations."[10] Roland nonetheless anticipated later scholarship by asking in his modest 150-page study many of the same questions posed by authors of today's new emancipation studies. He was in fact one of the earliest scholars to assess the transition from slave to free labor (what Roland termed "the etiquette of dealing with wage laborers"), to discuss the evolution of postwar labor contracts, and to note the determination of the freedpeople to hold their own land.

The reissue of *Louisiana Sugar Plantations During the Civil War* is especially timely because much of the best current work on slavery and the Civil War examines the emancipation process—how whites and blacks began to carve out new lives, new relationships, during the defining moment of wartime black liberation. Though the emancipation experience in Civil War Louisiana's

---

8. C. Peter Ripley, *Slaves and Freedmen in Civil War Louisiana* (Baton Rouge, 1976), 210–11.
9. Charles P. Roland, review of C. Peter Ripley's *Slaves and Freedmen in Civil War Louisiana* in *Louisiana History,* XIX (1978), 372.
10. Charles P. Roland to John David Smith, November 15, 1996, in possession of the author.

sugar region deserves a modern work, one incorporating new sources and the fruits of recent study, future scholars will want to begin their research by consulting Roland's accurate and insightful book. There is no better summary of the "winds of destruction"—to use Roland's words—that had "blown from friend and foe alike." This powerful gust resulted in the end of an era for Louisiana's planter elite.

John David Smith
North Carolina State University

LOUISIANA SUGAR PLANTATIONS DURING THE CIVIL WAR

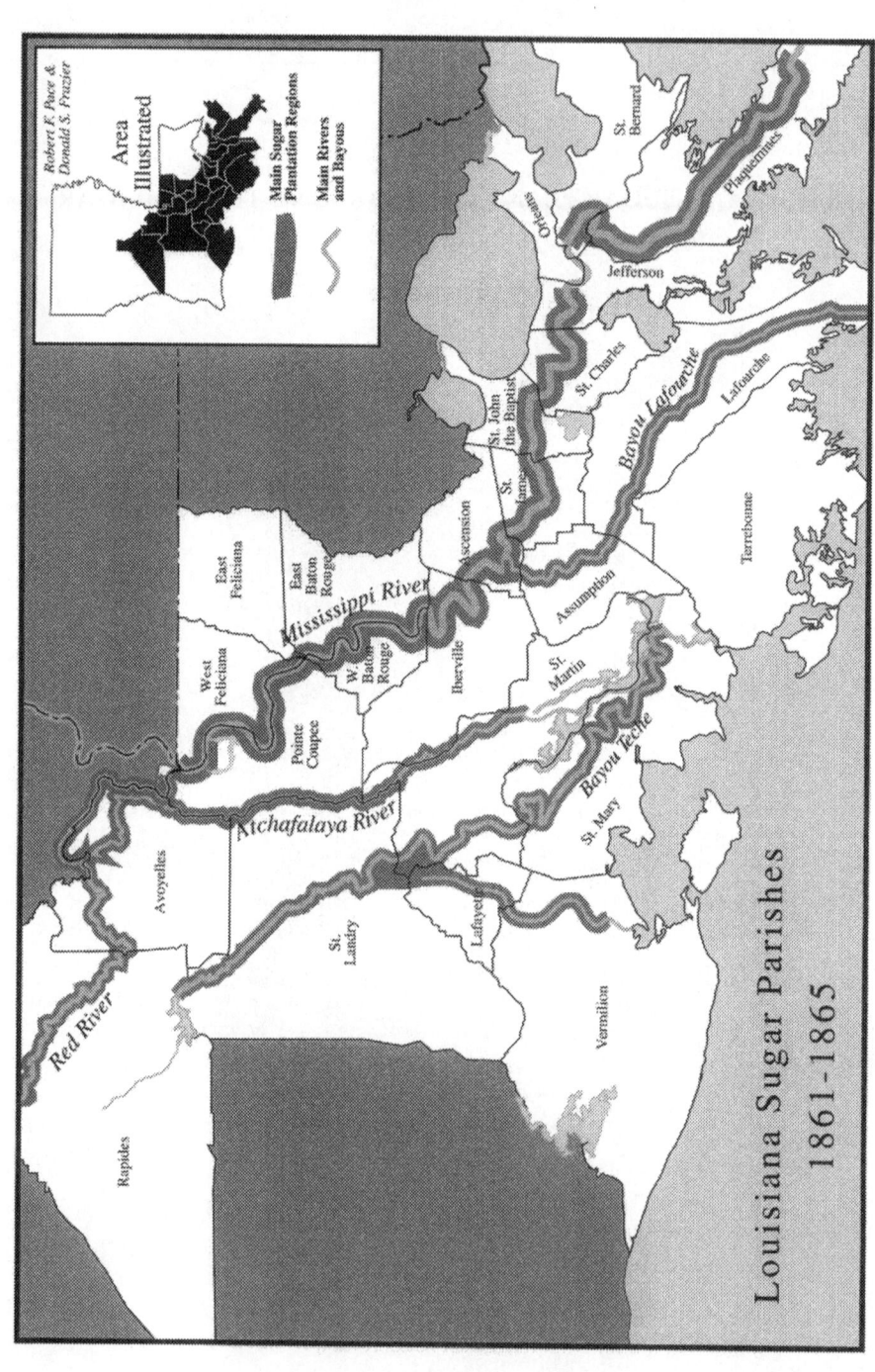

CHAPTER I

THE CANE COUNTRY

A favored and colorful part of the Old South was the Louisiana sugar country. This area was a labyrinthine river land of ample cane plantations interspersed with narrow sugar farms, of white-columned mansions contrasting with humble dwellings, of tall-chimneyed sugarhouses in juxtaposition with primitive mule-drawn cane mills, of Anglo-American planters among Creole proprietors, of Irish and "Cajun" laborers in the midst of a multitude of Negro slaves, and of affluent and graceful living in the presence of rural simplicity and back-breaking toil.

The cane country formed a crude triangle in lower Louisiana spreading from the Red River on the north to the marshes bordering the Gulf of Mexico on the south, and from the Mississippi River on the east to Bayou Vermilion on the west. Threading the land were four major streams and innumerable smaller ones. The Red River entered the sugar region at its northern point and flowed southeast to join the Mississippi over three hundred miles above the Gulf by way of a short "bridle" called Old River. The Atchafalaya River left the Mississippi through Old River, transected the cane land, and poured into the Gulf west of the debouchment of the parent stream. Bayou Lafourche diverged from the Mississippi below Old River, ran through the heart of the sugar area, and reached the Gulf at a point between the mouths of the Mississippi and the Atchafalaya. Bayou Teche, renowned for the Evangeline romance, had its source south of the lower Red River, proceeded through an expanse of the richest plantation country, and joined the Atchafalaya a few miles from the Gulf.

Plantation life in the sugar parishes[1] conformed closely with the demands of geography, two factors of which determined the growth of a riverbank society. These were the location of the arable land, and the importance of water transportation in a period before the use of the steam locomotive. The surface of the rivers and bayous was in most places higher than the surrounding land. Fertile soil spread away from the streams for depths that varied from a few hundred yards to several

---

[1] Sugar was cultivated in twenty-four Louisiana parishes in the pre-Civil War period.

miles. Behind the tillable land lay great wooded swamps into which drained the overflow waters of the rivers. Farms and plantations occupied the long, narrow ribbons of land between rivers and swamps. Every establishment fronted on a stream, and steamboats connected the planters with New Orleans.

Communications with the outside world were good. New Orleans was the great port of the sugar land, where planters sold their wares at the market on the levee, and ocean vessels took on cargo for distribution to Atlantic coastal communities. In New Orleans were located banks and firms of commission merchants that provided capital for the economy of the lower Mississippi Valley. Planters flocked to the city to purchase Yankee-produced machinery and supplies and to bid for Virginia and Carolina Negroes at the slave markets.

The plantation country along the Mississippi was called the "Coast." Southward from the mouth of the Red River, the Mississippi was lined with sugar estates of all sizes. As far down as Baton Rouge, occasional cotton plantations defied the sugar monopoly of the river bank, but below the capital city the triumph of cane was complete. A nineteenth century novelist described the Coast as "an almost continuous succession of sugarhouses, with their tall chimneys, surrounded by fields of green sugar cane, undulating in the blazing sun, like the miniature waves of an emerald sea."[1] This description would have applied to plantations along the other major waterways of lower Louisiana.

Sugar was first granulated in Louisiana on a profitable scale in 1795 by the Creole, Jean Etienne de Boré.[2] Within a few years after de Boré's initial experiments, political events took an important hand in shaping the career of the sugar industry. In 1803 Louisiana became a part of the United States, thereby placing the cane land within the limits of a swift-growing nation that provided an extensive home market for its produce. Creole planters should have gesticulated in delight if they had been aware that they had become part of a people who soon would be the world's greatest sugar eaters. Demand for sugar increased with rapid growth of the American population, and two vital barriers arose to ward off enemies of the cane growers. These were levees against the ruinous overflows of the Mississippi River and tariffs against West Indian competition. Hardier types of cane were introduced, and improved

---

[1] Thomas P. May, *The Earl of Mayfield* (Philadelphia, 1880), 65.

[2] J. Carlyle Sitterson, *Sugar Country; the Cane Industry in the South* (Lexington, 1953), 5. This volume records the definitive history of the Louisiana sugar industry.

agricultural techniques appeared. The sugar culture flourished and brought prosperity to the bayou land.

The Creole population at first formed a cultural wedge in the American community, but the rich soil of Louisiana attracted increasing numbers of American planters. These newcomers brought their own way of life with them, and within a few years cotton was challenging sugar for supremacy in lower Louisiana. This contest was short-lived, however, for settlers south of the Red River were shortly convinced that the climate was not favorable to cotton, and the typical American planter in that area soon shifted to cane.[1] By 1850 the transition was complete in the lower parishes. At the outbreak of the Civil War there were 1,291 cane plantations in operation,[2] and the economy of south Louisiana centered around the sugar industry.

The constitutive cell of the sugar civilization was the plantation. It was a farm where cane was grown, a factory where sugar was produced, and a home to the proprietor and his family and retinue of slaves. The nature of the sugar-making process prevented use of centrally located custom mills, with the result that every plantation, regardless of size, had its own sugarhouse. This was true of a little place on False River that in 1862 turned out only thirteen hogsheads of sugar as well as John Burnside's immense Houmas Plantation in Ascension Parish, which that same season produced 5,150 hogsheads.[3]

The center of gravity of the sugar industry lay in the large plantations. During the opening year of the Civil War, before the conflict affected the state's agricultural output, nearly one fourth of the sugar establishments turned out over 500 hogsheads each, and many grew 1,000 or more. That same year only about one seventh of the plantations produced less than 100 hogsheads each.[4] The advantage of the big plantation lay in the prohibitive cost of machinery, which was far above that required for the production of cotton. The average value of 1,000 sugarhouses was $50,000, and many cost over $100,000.[5] Machinery alone in the

---

[1] *Ibid.*, 27.

[2] P. A. Champomier, *Statement of the Sugar Crop Made in Louisiana in 1861-1862* (New Orleans, 1862), 39. Statements were published annually.

[3] *Ibid.*, 14. Hogsheads were casks of varying capacity. Champomier considered a hogshead to be 1,150 pounds of sugar.

[4] *Ibid.*, 1-38, *passim*.

[5] Walter Prichard, "The Effects of the Civil War on the Louisiana Sugar Industry," *Journal of Southern History* (Baton Rouge, Lexington), V (August, 1939), 317.

plant of Valcour Aime of St. James Parish was worth $60,000.[1] Sugar was not economically suited to small farming.

In approaching by steamboat a typical sugar plantation, one first saw "the house," the master's dwelling. It was an institution of the Southern scene glorified in literature and lore, and even today venerated in its dilapidation. Set well back from the levee, with lines softened by a columned façade, the white structure dominated its surroundings and lent an impressive elegance to the countryside. Within high-ceilinged rooms and shaded verandas flowed the domestic and social life of the plantation community. Like the manor house of an earlier day, it was and yet remains the highest symbol of the grandeur of the ante-bellum sugar civilization. Between levee and mansion spread the lawn, "level as a billiard table," and usually shaded by great live oaks and magnolias.

The sugarhouse was at a convenient point for transporting cane from the fields and hogsheads of sugar to the pier on the river. Numerous other buildings, including barn, stables, gristmill, icehouse, laundry, dairy, tannery, smithy, and hospital, were located about the premises. Back of the owner's house, or sometimes to one side, lay the "quarter," a row of whitewashed cabins housing Negro slaves. Behind the quarter spread great, flat fields of cane, the real treasure of the sugar region. Intersected by an elaborate grid of canals, the land drained surplus water into the swamp at the rear of the plantation, where often a second levee held out backwater. A bucket-wheel, driven by steam, dipped water from inside the back levee and poured it into the swamp beyond.[2]

The plantation ideal was supreme in lower Louisiana. This cannot be demonstrated statistically or scientifically, but it was unmistakable to the many travelers and writers who visited the state before the Civil War. New Orleans newspapers dedicated much of their space to planter activities, thoughts, and needs. Often men successful in other walks of life turned to sugar planting. The cases of Senator Judah P. Benjamin and Bishop Leonidas Polk illustrate the point. Critics of the plantation tradition denounce it as a myth, as much of it doubtless was. But myth can shape reality. The important point was that planters believed and participated in the tradition. The famous English war correspondent, William Howard Russell, hit the mark when he observed, "The more one sees of a planter's life the greater is the conviction that its charms

---

[1] Ulrich B. Phillips, *American Negro Slavery; a Survey of the Supply, Employment and Control of Negro Labor as Determined by the Plantation Regime* (New York, 1918), 243.

[2] John M. Mackie, *From Cape Cod to Dixie and the Tropics* (New York, 1864), 181.

come from a particular turn of mind...."[1] This "turn of mind," which could be called the creative myth, lent to the plantation community a vast sense of self-sufficiency and power. In the opinion of many witnesses, it generated warmth and grace. A great American scholar put the same idea in different form when he said that the vigor and poetry of Southern plantation life lay in its moral certainty of itself.[2]

The great sugar estates possessed a manorial atmosphere, a characteristic perfectly described by one bred in the plantation tradition: "So the Louisiana Planter, physicked, even scarified by his own physician, his soul saved by his own pastor, near his own dead in his own cemetery (let us hope they were not sent there by the first mentioned), drawn to the door by his own mettled steeds; gazing between naps through the window at his liberal pastures where grazed his blooded stock and beyond that, ten to one with the odds in his favor at the perfect oval of his private race track, and the miles of... cane in his vast fields, was indeed 'Monarch of all he surveyed.'"[3] If this account be disqualified on the ground that the writer was overcome with nostalgia, it may be compared with that of a highly realistic contemporary journalist, who pictured the sugar planter as a seventeenth-century lord in his great hall.[4]

The section's network of rivers and bayous provided easy transportation and gave the sugar land a feeling of solidarity perhaps stronger than in other parts of the South. Not enough cane proprietors lived in New Orleans to form an urbanized, absentee planter class. The role of the Mississippi in making it possible for Creole landowners to reside on their estates and at the same time enjoy much of the social life of New Orleans was doubtless important in keeping the city from becoming another Versailles.

Plantation women held the key position in home activities. The stereotype of the langorous Southern girl, swooning fashionably and sighing away her time while a faithful servant brushed at the flies, was an amusing fiction. The planter's wife was a busy woman. Her duties as mother, hostess, commander and tutor of the household slaves, and sometime keeper of accounts marked her as a woman of keen intelligence and resolute character. Observers might quarrel with every other aspect

---

[1] William Howard Russell, *My Diary North and South* (Boston, 1863), 285.
[2] Henry Adams, *The Education of Henry Adams* (New York, 1931), 246.
[3] Louise Butler, "The Louisiana Planter and His Home," *Louisiana Historical Quarterly* (New Orleans), X (July, 1927), 357.
[4] Russell, *My Diary North and South*, 263.

of the Southern scene, but one of the severest critics of the slavery regime paid Southern women the high compliment of saying that they were "unexcelled in the world for every quality which command[ed] respect, admiration, and love." [1] The electric shock of the mistress' personality charged the plantation home with its boasted vitality and graciousness.

Sugar planters were men of responsibility. In local government and administration they were comparable to the squires of Elizabethan England. Wealth and extensive property would have gone far in making them leaders, but affluence was not the sole factor. In appraising the cane growers, the predominance of the plantation ideal must be held in mind. Personality and the rare genius of common sense were powerful elements in giving them their place in the community. A significant cementing agent in white society was the presence of a multitude of Negro slaves in the sugar parishes. Planter, small farmer, and townsman shared a common interest in standing superior to the human chattel, and the great proprietor, often owner of scores of slaves, was the logical one to command. Sugar cultivators served as judges, overseers for the poor, district road commissioners, school commissioners, police jurymen, grand jurymen, church vestrymen, and in many other positions of local authority. [2] At higher levels they sat in Congress and in the Governor's chair at Baton Rouge. The sugar grower's time was not monopolized in riding a thoroughbred over his estate and sipping mint juleps.

In the lives of many cane proprietors religion was not a compelling force, for perhaps they were more nearly able to achieve a "heaven on earth" than was the general run of mankind. The large Creole element was unanimously Catholic, while American planters were distributed among the leading Protestant faiths, with the older plantation stock from Virginia and the Carolinas leaning toward Episcopalianism. One sugar grower was bluntly agnostic, sneering that some people thought that a man "could not... be honest unless a professor of Religion—in other words a church goer, Bah!" The death of this landowner's wife in 1848 caused him to sigh: "Dreary is my lot, the world is cold and selfish, if I could only Believe we were to meet hereafter would give me great relive." [3] Some planters attended services at their conven-

---

[1] Frederick Law Olmsted, *A Journey in the Seaboard Slave States; with Remarks on Their Economy* (New York, 1856), 509.

[2] Edwin Adams Davis, *Plantation Life in the Florida Parishes of Louisiana, 1836-1846, as Reflected in the Diary of Bennet H. Barrow* (New York, 1943), 65.

[3] *Ibid.*, 66.

ience, made routine contributions to the cause, occasionally played host to the minister, and enjoyed the church as a social as well as religious outlet.

The difficulty of appraising the cane cultivator's true attitude on slavery is complicated by the problem of his talking one way and sometimes acting another. Many owners of scores of Negroes condemned slavery in the abstract, while they outbid their neighbors at the New Orleans slave marts. An observer found both Creole and American sugar growers who deprecated the institution as uneconomical and morally debasing, but felt that they were not responsible for it, could do nothing about it, and must make the best of it.[1] Others followed the traditional Southern line in hailing "the peculiar institution" a boon to white and black alike. To one onlooker, sugar planters were "anthropo-proprietors" who consigned the Negro to the position of chattel "because [his] skull [would not] hold as many ounces of shot as the white man's."[2]

Absorbing political issues of the mid-nineteenth century caught Louisiana cane growers between fires. As slave owners they were urged to support the Democratic Party, which appeared to offer greater security to slavery. On the other hand, unlike the anti-tariff cotton planters of the South, sugar producers were indebted to the Federal government for a tariff against Cuban competition. This, plus the hope of Federal aid in constructing and maintaining levees, made most sugar planters nationalist in sentiment and won them to the Whig Party.[3]

A robust social life gave verve and color to the sugar land. The great landowners loved good horseflesh, and many of the more elaborate establishments had racecourses. Duncan Kenner of St. James Parish possessed a fine stable of race horses and brood mares under the care of an English horseman. Kenner was a well-known figure at the tracks of New Orleans and Charleston. William and Bennet H. Barrow of West Feliciana Parish at one time owned some of the best animals in the country, as did William J. Minor of Natchez, Mississippi, proprietor of three Louisiana sugar plantations. These and other planters, highly enthusiastic over the thrilling sport, subscribed to racing periodicals and kept trained jockeys in their retinues.[4]

---

[1] Olmsted, *A Journey in the Seaboard Slave States*, 675-676.
[2] Russell, *My Diary North and South*, 266.
[3] Sitterson, *Sugar Country*, 88. See also Roger W. Shugg, *Origins of Class Struggle in Louisiana; a Social History of White Farmers and Laborers during Slavery and after, 1840-1875* (Baton Rouge, 1939), 4.
[4] Russell, *My Diary North and South*, 286.

Plantation social life reached its pinnacle in the great balls that occasionally lit the mansions, when nightlong dancing and sumptuous festivities were in order. A landowner's diary captured the fierce gaiety of one of these affairs: "Got a violin player from 'Town.' ... Let them rest & Knap during the day sometimes. Playing smut—at dark began to dance, at 12 Oclock their consciences made them refuse to dance any longer, it being Saturday night, to punish them fastened the doors 'till near two ok some blew the Lights out others tried to get out the windows, any thing, but dance they would'ent retired at 2 ok all nearly broke down, never have seen a collection so sudden and so perfectly free easy & happy for two days & nights, All restraint thrown aside never enjoyed myself as much." [1]

Outstanding events in the social life of the bayou land were the sugarhouse parties that were featured during the sugar-making season. These were frolics held in the sugarhouses, during which plantation sons and daughters danced, played games, sang, and stuffed on pralines and pecans dipped in molasses on the spot.[2]

In addition to these major events, there were many lesser amusements. Riding to the hounds was popular with some inhabitants. Many planters favored hunting bear and deer at night in the swamps. Fishing parties, including outdoor fish fries, were preferred by others.[3] Christmas was a universal day of feasting and eggnog parties, and weddings were superbly festive. The "dignified pilgrimages" of planter families to church on Sundays often were of as great social significance as they were of religious purpose. Even funerals occasionally were attended by invitation only, with notices written on paper decorated with heavy black bars and a minute scene of setting sun, leaning tombstone, and weeping willows.[4]

Though the plantations were the stage for most of the proprietors' social performances, not all activities occurred there. New Orleans was the entertainment Mecca of lower Louisiana, and many sugar planters kept town houses in the city for the season of opera and balls. Resorts on the Gulf were visited seasonally by plantation folk for boating, eating sea food, and frolicking. The journey down the Mississippi from planta-

---

[1] Davis, *Plantation Life in the Florida Parishes of Louisiana*, 53.
[2] Butler, "The Louisiana Planter and His Home," *Louisiana Historical Quarterly*, X (July, 1927), 361.
[3] Davis, *Plantation Life in the Florida Parishes of Louisiana*, 57.
[4] Work Projects Administration, *Louisiana; a Guide to the State* (New York, 1941), 109.

tion to city was a pleasure jaunt. Steamboats with glamor in their names, such as *Diana* and *Sultana*, catered to landowners with bars, ballrooms, and rich cuisine. A planter family boarding a vessel usually encountered numerous friends having the same destination. Dancing, dining, flirting, tippling, cigar smoking, card playing, and gossiping filled the day. Ostentatious proprietors were said to have thrown silver dollars at floating targets in the river, wagering on their aim. Legend has it that one flashy entrepreneur lit expensive cigars with ten-dollar bills.[1]

Cane planters lived full lives. They strove with a measure of success to build a graceful society on a foundation of sugar cane and Negro slavery. Activities centered on the plantation, except for occasional journeys to New Orleans, the great economic and social hub of the region. Sugar proprietors sat in councils at local, state, and national levels, discharging their duties with a competence and honesty doubtless equal to that of other groups in positions of like responsibility. They were men of sound wit who tempered their lives with vigorous play, set the pace for the area in which they lived, and made the plantation ideal supreme.

---

[1] Butler, "The Louisiana Planter and His Home," *Louisiana Historical Quarterly*, X (July, 1927), 362.

CHAPTER II

THE PECULIAR INSTITUTION AND PLANTATION ROUTINE

Negro slaves were the laboring force of the sugar plantations and the base of the social pyramid in the black belt parishes. A contemporary student of the cane industry estimated the number of slaves to be 139,000.[1] Treatment of workers in the sugar area was probably as humane as elsewhere in the South, notwithstanding a current opinion to the contrary. It was said in the upper South that the average life of a Negro in the cane country was only seven years. Perhaps slave owners in the cotton land nurtured the story that "selling down the river" was an especially grim punishment primarily as a disciplinary device, just as Louisiana masters sometimes threatened their own recalcitrant laborers with the fate of being shipped to Cuba.

The black population of the cane plantation inhabited a village of cabins, constructed of brick or wood according to the means and disposition of the owner, and customarily set at a distance behind the mansion. A critical observer of the 1850's found that slave quarters on Mississippi River estates were as good, if not superior, to those of mill operatives in New England.[2] He felt that clothes and rations were adequate, if not modish or tasty, and was favorably impressed by generous allowances of tobacco. The sheer economic interest of the owner in his thralls has been pointed up repeatedly as the great factor discouraging ill treatment of the blacks, and this undoubtedly was an important aspect of master-slave relations. A statement by a plantation overseer in 1861 to the effect that he feared to put the Negroes to work in the rain because if they "got wet or caught cold [they] would be apt to die" was charged with about as much compassion as that of a piney woods farmer for the welfare of his mules.[3] But the stark financial implications of humaneness under the slavery regime have sometimes been over-

---

[1] Henry Latham, *Black and White; a Journal of a Three Months' Tour in the United States* (London, 1867), 171.
[2] Olmsted, *A Journey in the Seaboard Slave States*, 660.
[3] P. S. Hamilton to Charles Mathews, August 14, 1861, Charles Mathews and Family Papers (Department of Archives, Louisiana State University, Baton Rouge).

stressed, for in many cases owners felt a personal concern for their servants.[1]

The cane plantation served as a school where the untrained Negro learned techniques of farming and household routine, and where he assimilated elements of the white man's culture, including religion, language, myths, conceits, and habits. Discipline was by the whip. In an age when all school children sat under the shadow of the teacher's rod, planter's felt little or no pangs of conscience in authorizing overseers to administer lashes. They did, however, hedge these whippings with restrictions designed to prevent wanton brutality. William J. Minor, Terrebonne and Ascension Parish cane grower, counseled his manager not to break the skin in punishing Negroes and never to discipline one while in passion, for fear of overdoing the matter. The action was to be taken in seriousness and "a gentlemanly manner," since the culprit must be made to appreciate that he was being chastised for bad conduct, and not out of a spirit of revenge, anger, or caprice.[2] Overseers often were prohibited from using the whip except in the presence of the master. But not all owners were this scrupulous, and many cases of barbarity occurred.

Numerous planters encouraged religion among their slaves. Negroes belonging to Creole masters were Catholic, while those owned by Americans tended to follow the Protestant choice of the individual proprietor. Episcopal Bishop Leonidas Polk, a Lafourche Parish sugar grower, insisted that his Negroes be Episcopalians. House workers often attended services with the planter's family, sitting in a special place in the building. Field hands might be permitted their own exhorter, but more often they listened to the sermons of a minister sent among them by the master.[3]

Some owners felt no need for religious instruction among their human chattels. William J. Minor charged his overseer that no preaching of any sort be permitted on the plantation and that the Negroes not be granted passes to attend exhortations elsewhere.[4] A traveler in the cane

---

[1] Sitterson, *Sugar Country*, 96.

[2] William J. Minor Plantation Diary (1861-1865), rules for overseer (Department of Archives, Louisiana State University). Five separate volumes of the William J. Minor Plantation Diary (1847-1870) cited in this study include entries dated 1861-1862, 1861-1865, 1861-1868, 1863, and 1863-1868.

[3] See, for example, Bayside Plantation Journal (1846-1866), September 29, 1861 (Microfilm copy in possession of author. Original in Southern Historical Collection, University of North Carolina Library, Chapel Hill).

[4] Minor Plantation Diary (1861-1865), rules for overseer.

region discovered that owners often flouted the state law prohibiting slaves to be worked on Sundays.[1] The famous English war correspondent, William Howard Russell, encountered Negro boys of nine and ten years of age who had never been in a church nor even heard the name of Jesus Christ. The overseer explained apologetically that it was not "right to put these things into their heads so young." He was of the opinion that religious teaching disturbed their minds and led them astray. When questioned as to what occurred when slaves died, he pointed to a nearby field where they were buried, explaining that some of them had "a sort of prayers" as funeral services.[2] An evangelist in lower Louisiana in 1857 was aghast at the great number of Negroes who never entered a chapel nor heard a sermon, and he declared that spiritually the sugar land fitted the prophet's vision of "dry bones in a valley."[3]

The large plantations played a role not far removed from that of the present welfare state. On some places Negro infants were born under the care of the plantation doctor and throughout life had access to a hospital located near the quarter. Day nurseries might provide for young children during working hours, while the mother was at her appointed tasks, with specified times set aside for suckling. The usual plan for the slave hospital was that the proprietor engaged a physician on contract to make periodic visits to the plantation. William J. Minor ordered his overseer to give special attention to sick laborers, to see that they had all necessary conveniences, and to enforce rigidly the doctor's directions "in every particular."[4]

No feature of slavery has been more strongly emphasized by its apologists than the old-age security of the Negroes. On establishments of conscientious masters, this doubtless was one of its brighter aspects. The old, worn-out Negroes of such a place were said to be its heirlooms, and all large sugar domains possessed a number of these superannuated hangers-on, "dosing into eternity" in the evening of life.[5]

Planters acted as judges in settling disputes among the slaves. Trades, contracts, and partnerships appeared on a simple and informal basis in the quarter, requiring arbitration and settlement. Repression of vice called for the owner to exercise local police authority. Friends of slavery

---

[1] Olmsted, *A Journey in the Seaboard Slave States*, 651.
[2] Russell, *My Diary North and South*, 275.
[3] *De Bow's Review* (New Orleans), XXIX (September, 1860), 367-368.
[4] Minor Plantation Diary (1861-1868), rules for overseer.
[5] Russell, *My Diary North and South*, 256.

implored masters to promote permanent marriages and disallow divorce, but many owners were prone to overlook promiscuity in the quarter. One planter ordered that a month's notice of intention to marry be given by both parties, and divorce was permitted on his plantations only after a similar warning. His chief deterrent to separation was the requirement that divorced parties could not remarry without agreeing to receive twenty-five lashes "well laid on... unless they had agreed to take that number for the privilege of parting."[1]

Slave organization has been compared with that of an army. The master was the commander, and the overseer his lieutenant. From the overseer the chain of command ran through first and second drivers, who performed the functions of sergeants, to the common hands—the private soldiers of the slave company. The plantation bell was to the Negroes what the bugle is to troops. It was rung in the morning by the first driver as the quarter's reveille; meals were announced by its tolling; and at night it sounded taps to send the laborers to their cabins.

The position of overseer called for a man of great versatility, patience, and common sense. Not only did the second-in-command discharge discipline and manage the Negroes, but he was held generally responsible for the running of the entire establishment. Two or three times a week he conducted a bed check of the cabins at night after the ringing of the retirement bell. The first driver was required to make a similar inspection every night and deliver a report to the overseer in the field the next morning. To the overseer went blacks seeking permission to leave the plantation, and he granted or refused passes at his discretion. Nonresident Negroes coming to visit the plantation applied to him and presented passes from their home managers. In the absence of the owner, the overseer kept the journal, account book, and a book of Negro births and deaths. Mechanics and other specialists on the place made periodic reports to him regarding the condition of their machinery and equipment, and these were verified by personal investigation.[2]

Drivers were Negroes chosen for their intelligence, industry, and qualities of leadership. They set the pace in the field, checked the quarters, supervised all types of labor, and exercised disciplinary powers over the other slaves. The delegation of such authority to Negroes entailed dangers, and one planter cautioned his first driver that he should conduct himself in an exemplary manner so that "there [would] be no complaints

---

[1] Minor Plantation Diary (1861-1865), rules for overseer.
[2] Minor Plantation Diary (1861-1868), rules for overseer.

of his being too intimate with the wives and daughters of the other men." If this subordinate should attempt to lord it over the laborers in an arrogant manner, "burnt brandy should not save him from the most severe punishment." [1]

Skilled personnel were required to carry on activities subsidiary to growing cane and making sugar, and every efficient sugar plantation boasted a host of trained specialists. A visitor was surprised at finding Negro carpenters and masons building a new sugarhouse on one establishment. [2] But a closer investigation would have revealed that on many large estates Negroes were instructed in sugar making, cobbling, brickmaking, and wagonmaking. The retinue of skilled laborers was rounded out by blacksmiths, coopers, mechanics, engineers, tanners, millers, and cartmen. Although slaves performed all of these services on some places, white men were engaged on others, and during the 1850's, as sugar-making apparatus advanced in complexity, demand for white experts measurably increased. [3]

On the eve of the Civil War slave prices soared to $1,800 for prime field hands, and planters were loath to commit such expensive servants to the more hazardous tasks on their plantations. Instead, they hired Irish immigrant laborers to dig ditches and canals, level forests, and clear waste land. One overseer, though concerned at the high wages of free labor, hastened to point out, "It was much better to have Irish to do it, who cost nothing to the planter, if they died, than to use up good field hands in such severe employment." [4] Landowners often hired additional hands during the grinding season, since more labor was required to make sugar than to grow cane. When this became necessary, planters paid 'Cajun" farmers by the day to work in the harvest. [5]

Slavery theoretically provided the blacks with subsistence, giving them food, clothing, and shelter in return for their labor. Actually, planters found it to their interest to bestow gifts at intervals as inducement to superior performance. The custom on numerous plantations was to distribute money at Christmas to each industrious family, with other bonuses from time to time to individual slaves to let them know that

---

[1] *Ibid.*, duties of first driver.
[2] Russell, *My Diary North and South*, 273.
[3] V. Alton Moody, *Slavery on Louisiana Sugar Plantations* (New Orleans, 1924), 55.
[4] Russell, *My Diary North and South*, 273.
[5] Moody, *Slavery on Louisiana Sugar Plantations*, 59.

the master appreciated their efforts.[1] Of more substantial benefit to the Negroes were garden plots in which each family could cultivate vegetables to supplement the customary ration. Masters frequently permitted their laborers to hunt, fish, collect driftwood, pick moss, and hire themselves out in order to earn spending money.

Native ingenuity, coupled with sublime disregard for the sanctity of property, added to the workers' income. Petty traders thronged the Mississippi in boats, coasting in to shore under cover of darkness, and trafficking with the blacks. Pipes and other machinery from the sugarhouses made excellent material for barter, and planters complained bitterly that these "chicken thief" merchants could induce the Negroes to steal anything in exchange for a drink or some bauble.[2]

Slaves enjoyed amusements consistent with their low place in the social scale. Sundays were usually days of rest, except in the grinding season, while on plantations where religion was encouraged, worship services offered an avenue of social expression. Unless conditions in field and sugarhouse made grinding imperative, Christmas was a day of festivity for bondsman as well as master. On Christmas Day of 1860, while the owner of a Bayou Teche plantation feasted in his mansion, his Negroes sank their teeth into roast pork contributed by him to enliven their holiday.[3] The year's social high light for the slaves was a rousing sugarhouse dinner and ball at the end of the grinding period. These diversions, scattered at intervals among periods of grueling toil, were water in the desert to the fun-loving Negroes and did much to buoy up their spirits.

Sugar agriculture was a cycle of planting, hoeing, plowing, and cutting. In January seed cane saved from the previous season's yield was planted in furrows laid open by double mouldboard plows. For this operation the field force was organized into different gangs. One brought cane by armfuls from the carts and dropped it by the furrows; the second placed it in the ground with two or three stalks parallel; and the third used broad-bladed hoes to cover it with a layer of soil. When the young cane appeared above ground the earth was carefully plowed away from the shoots, and throughout spring and summer hoe gangs were busy scraping grass. By July the cane stood five or six feet high. Wide furrows between the cane beds were kept clean of grass so that they

---
[1] Olmsted, *A Journey in the Seaboard Slave States*, 660.
[2] *Ibid.*, 674-675.
[3] Bayside Plantation Journal, December 25, 1860.

would drain surplus rain water into the canals designed to carry it into the swamp.

Planters were at the mercy of the weather in harvesting, for the Louisiana growing season was too short for the cane to mature thoroughly. Cultivators were caught between a desire to delay cutting in order to get a greater sugar content and the necessity of grinding before ruinous frosts descended upon them. October was the usual month to begin harvesting. Cutting gangs, armed with great knives, advanced into the fields and leveled the cane. On some places seed cane was planted as soon as it was cut; on others it was "mattressed," to await planting at the end of the grinding season. This process consisted of laying the cane unstripped of leaves in "mattresses," or "mats," and covering it with earth to protect it from the climate. Cutting for the mill was a routine of four strokes of the blade to each cane. Two sweeping vertical blows stripped it of leaves, a horizontal movement cut it at the ground, and a final chop took off the top. Mule carts then transported it to the sugarhouse.

As long as the weather was favorable, cutting, hauling, and sugar making went on simultaneously. The first frost caused many planters to "windrow" the threatened cane. This was the hurried cutting of the remainder of the crop so that it might be laid unstripped in the furrows, where it had additional protection against cold until it could be ground. When the cane was windrowed, grinding went on day and night in a Herculean effort to save as much of the harvest as possible.[1]

The sugarhouse was the industrial nerve center of the plantation. There the juice was ground from the cane between great iron rollers. Impurities were strained from the raw juice, which then passed through a series of open kettles, each with a French name, such as the "grande," the "flambeau," the "sirop," and the "batterie," until it cooked to crystallization. An application of lime brought remaining impurities to the top in the form of scum, which was dipped off with ladles, and the mother liquid was placed in shallow pans for cooling and granulation. It then was scooped into hogsheads and stored in a spacious room in the sugarhouse, where for several days it continued to drain through holes left in the great containers for that purpose. This liquid ran into great vats, called cisterns, from which it was removed and barreled for

---

[1] Ulrich B. Phillips, *Life and Labor in the Old South* (Boston, 1929), 121. See also Olmsted, *A Journey in the Seaboard Slave States*, 665-666.

sale as molasses. The hogsheads were refilled with sugar and made ready for shipment.[1]

During the 1840's and 1850's the larger plantations installed machinery that improved sugar quality and increased processing efficiency. Vacuum pans—closed retorts for steam condensing—permitted boiling at lower temperature, thereby reducing the amount of molasses by-product and bringing forth a superior grade of sugar. A method was discovered whereby dried cane pulp, called "bagasse," could be used as fuel. A further economy and improvement resulted from the "Rillieux" invention for employing vapor from one vacuum pan to heat the other pan. Quality was enhanced by the introduction of filters in which the syrup passed through bone black, which strained out any remaining impurities and bleached the product.[2]

The grinding season brought slaves to the most unremitting labor of the year. An observer found that during this period every able-bodied man, woman, and child on a Mississippi River plantation, including overseer and owner, worked fully eighteen hours a day. From October until January sugar making was seldom broken, and fires under the boilers never went out. Laborers worked in shifts, with three quarters of them constantly at their stations, and no man got more than six hours of rest out of twenty-four.[3]

Bayside Plantation on the Teche revealed a normal master's carefully planned routine and allocation of labor during the sugar-making season. Early October of 1860 found the slaves mattressing seed cane, making barrels, and preparing hogsheads to receive sugar. When the cane was mattressed all workers went into the sugarhouse to ready machinery for grinding. Hauling began on October 11, and from that time forward the hands were divided between field and sugarhouse, as the situation demanded, in such a way as to maintain the proper balance between cutting and grinding.[4]

Rigorous as was the toil of the harvest, the blacks apparently enjoyed that season more than any other. Masters boosted their morale with generous portions of food, whiskey, tobacco, and coffee, giving the entire process an atmosphere of frolic.[5]

---

[1] Sitterson, *Sugar Country*, 140-144.
[2] Lewis C. Gray, *History of Agriculture in the Southern United States to 1860*, 2 vols. (Washington, 1933), II, 741-742.
[3] Olmsted, *A Journey in the Seaboard Slave States*, 668.
[4] Bayside Plantation Journal, October 2 to December 5, 1860, *passim*.
[5] Olmsted, *A Journey in the Seaboard Slave States*, 668.

Planting cane and making sugar were the primary tasks on the plantation, but they were by no means all of the chores. Cane planters made at least a partial effort to attain self-sufficiency for their estates. A representative sugar establishment grew corn, hay, peas, beans, Irish potatoes, and yams, in addition to supporting herds of beef and milch cattle, swine, oxen, mules, horses, and sheep.[1] The Negroes devoted most of their time, other than in planting and harvesting cane, to the care of these subsidiary products. Even with this, their work was not done. Wood for the boiler had to be cut from the swamp, or fished from the river in the form of driftwood. Constant repairs on the levee were required, and plantation roads demanded close attention. This was an exceptionally onerous chore during the grinding season, when overuse and inclement weather frequently converted these cart trails into bottomless quagmires.[2]

Operating a cane plantation called for a high degree of coordination between agriculture and manufacture. Expensive machinery and Negroes were essential to the production of sugar. Upon the overseer fell the responsibility of keeping personnel on schedule and apparatus in condition, while proprietors strove to harmonize all elements of their establishments in order to achieve as full a measure of efficiency as possible.

---

[1] United States Census Returns, 1860, Schedule IV, Agriculture (Microfilm copy in the Hill Memorial Library, Louisiana State University. Original in the Duke University Library, Durham). This generalization is based upon examination of the production reports of several hundred sugar plantations.

[2] See, for example, Bayside Plantation Journal, September 2-24, 1860, *passim*.

CHAPTER III

SECESSION AND FARAWAY WAR

When the secession crisis came upon the South the mind of the sugar country presented a complete spectrum of opinion on the issue. A decade earlier the majority of large sugar producers had been Whigs, deeply grounded in nationalist sentiment. Many of them never fully accepted secession, and remained Unionist to the end. Events of the late 1850's, on the other hand, caused numerous cane planters to shift allegiance to the Democratic Party, where they felt lay a firmer sympathy for slave owners. At one pole of thought were the secessionists; at the other stood the Unionists. Perhaps the majority of the sugar proprietors fell somewhere between the two and awaited the unfolding of events before coming to the final fatal decision.

The Charleston convention of the Democratic Party in 1860 brought painfully into the open this polarity in the thinking of the cane planters. When William L. Yancy of Alabama bolted the convention, most of the Louisiana delegation followed him from the hall. But two members at first refused to leave. The leader of the withdrawing Louisiana group —ex-Governor Alexander Mouton—was a prominent sugar grower, and so was James McHatton of East Baton Rouge Parish, one of the two Louisiana delegates who remained and thereby signified disapproval of the drastic action that ultimately led down the dark corridor of secession. Thus in miniature was enacted the great political conflict raging in the cane land, as Mouton, the "Creole Hotspur," strode from the room denouncing McHatton with angry words and accusing finger.[1]

The presidential election of 1860 sharpened the clash of ideas among sugar planters. The political situation along Bayou Lafourche was an excellent example of this discord, as the sugar-dominated parishes of Ascension, Assumption, and Lafourche went for Stephen A. Douglas— providing a clear Unionist mandate—while the Pugh family, among the greatest of Bayou Lafourche planters, were zealous Breckinridge support-

---

[1] Eliza McHatton Ripley, *From Flag to Flag; A Woman's Adventures and Experiences in the South During the War, in Mexico, and in Cuba* (New York, 1889), 47. The two recalcitrant delegates, McHatton and Charles Jones, ultimately, under protest, acted with the majority of the Louisiana delegation. Jefferson Davis Bragg, *Louisiana in the Confederacy* (Baton Rouge, 1941), 10.

ers. A. Franklin and W. W. Pugh strove unsuccessfully to defeat Douglas by conducting political barbecues throughout the disaffected parishes.[1] Six lower sugar parishes supported John Bell, revealing along with those for Douglas an unmistakable Unionist sentiment, but the northern and western cane parishes voted for Breckinridge, who carried the state. A majority of the sugar parishes endorsed the extreme pro-slavery stand in the election, and thereby served as an augury of what the area would do in the crisis that was almost upon it.[2]

Presidential election day in November of 1860 caused no convulsion in the cane country; a St. Mary Parish planter appeared more interested in the purchase of two new boilers and in the progress of sugar making than in the momentous political events of the hour.[3] From the day of Lincoln's election until the end of the year was the incubation period of secession fever, however, and Louisiana planters watched grimly the withdrawal of South Carolina from the Union. Taut as a fiddle string, A. Franklin Pugh quadrupled his cigar smoking as he awaited word from other states.[4]

The Louisiana legislature set January 23, 1861, as the date for the meeting of a state convention to decide the secession question. Between the day of the presidential election and that of the meeting of the convention, the secessionist element among the cane cultivators began to come to the front. On December 27 Effingham Lawrence of Plaquemines Parish addressed in "forcible, eloquent and impressive language" a meeting of the Friends of Southern Rights and Separate State Secession, an organization whose title revealed its platform of action. Lawrence dwelt upon the long forbearance of the South under alleged Northern provocation, claiming that it was the right and duty of the region to "stand to her honor." He felt that the section should seek the equality with which she came into the Union, but of which in his opinion she had been deprived. "The duty of Louisiana and every citizen thereof," cried the great cane planter, "is to stand and defend Louisiana through fire and blood if necessary."[5] He little realized the prophecy of his words.

---

[1] A. Franklin Pugh Plantation Diary (1850, 1859-1863), October 28, 1860 (Department of Archives, Louisiana State University).

[2] Willie Malvin Caskey, *Secession and Restoration of Louisiana* (Baton Rouge, 1938), 14.

[3] William T. Palfrey Plantation Diary (1842-1895), November 6, 1860 (Department of Archives, Louisiana State University).

[4] Pugh Plantation Diary, January 5, 1861.

[5] New Orleans *Daily Crescent*, December 27, 1860.

The Pughs of the Bayou Lafourche region, though surrounded by conservatives, plunged with vigor into the task of sending secessionists to the convention. A. Franklin Pugh exulted over the news that New Orleans would send a majority of secessionist delegates—a sufficient number to carry the state out of the Union. "Well done Mobilians, ... well done Louisiana," he exclaimed. "Let the Yankees take care of themselves and ever after this hold their peace about the affairs of Louisiana."[1] Four days later Pugh commented more soberly on the seizure of Federal forts in Louisiana by state troops. He felt that the step had been wise, but cautioned with a flash of foresight, "We must keep what is left of Uncle Sam at arm's length or he may do us some harm." In his opinion the taking of the forts made secession inevitable; the step could not be retraced, and the cane proprietor was supremely happy over the outlook.[2]

Louisiana sugar cultivators led the movement that carried the state into secession.[3] Thirteen of the twenty-three parishes of the cane land were represented in the secession convention in January by immediate secessionist delegates. Among this number were the great sugar parishes of Iberville, St. Mary, Plaquemines, St. Bernard, St. Martin, and St. Charles. Nine sugar parishes sent cooperationist delegates, many of whom advocated secession in some form, but opposed immediate separation and had other questions as to method. Some of them called for further attempts at reconciliation with the North—such as constitutional amendments guaranteeing slavery—and felt that if these efforts should fail, the Southern states should withdraw in a bloc. Most of the cooperationists, however, favored immediate cooperative secession, in which all slaveholding states would withdraw together and form a Southern Union.[4]

The convention, meeting in Baton Rouge, was dominated by sugar growers. Effingham Lawrence called the meeting to order; John Moore, sugar producer and judge from St. Mary Parish, nominated ex-Governor Alexander Mouton as president, and the convention immediately elected to the post the sugar-planting "Creole Hotspur" of the ill-fated Charleston

---

[1] Pugh Plantation Diary, January 8, 1861.
[2] *Ibid.*, January 12, 1861.
[3] James K. Greer, "Louisiana Politics, 1845-1861," *Louisiana Historical Quarterly*, XIII (October, 1930), 643. See also Lane C. Kendall, "The Interregnum in Louisiana in 1861," *Louisiana Historical Quarterly*, XVI (July, 1933), 395-396.
[4] Kendall, "The Interregnum in Louisiana in 1861," *Louisiana Historical Quarterly*, XVI (July, 1933), 395.

convention. The determination of the secessionist group was expressed in President Mouton's opening words: "We are engaged in an important cause, the cause of a brave, loyal and enlightened people asserting their rights. I trust that, with the help of God, [we] will be able to carry them out." [1] They were indeed able to carry them out, and Louisiana was voted out of the Union. Two cooperationist attempts to stay immediate, separate Louisiana secession failed, and after these efforts were rejected most of the cooperationists swung into line for immediate secession, with the result that the measure passed by the overwhelming majority of 113 to 17. [2]

The men who took this fatal step were primarily great slave owners, whose motivating thought doubtless was a desire to protect the "peculiar institution." The New Orleans *Daily True Delta* claimed that the Louisiana secessionist delegates collectively owned more Negroes than any other political convention of equal number in the entire South. A. Franklin Pugh solemnly wrote a panegyric to those who had risked the action, "All honor to the men, who had the courage to take this first step, to prosperity which will be as permanent as earthly things may be." [3]

News of the decision created varied emotions, for not everyone rejoiced. A chronicler of those fevered days recalled, "Prophets arose in our midst, with vigorous tongue and powerful eloquence lifting the veil and giving us glimpses of the fiery sword suspended over our heads; but the pictures revealed were like pages in history, in which we had no part not lot, so hard was it for people who had for generations walked the flowery paths of peace, to realize war and all that that terrible word imports." [4]

Forecasters of gloom were drowned out in the exclamations of enthusiasm that arose from the bayou country. The Arlington Plantation household near Baton Rouge reflected this excitement as they gaily fashioned a Confederate flag of red flannel, white cotton cloth, and blue denim, and ran it up on an improvised flagstaff on the levee. Around it they danced, singing and shouting "in exuberance of spirit," as a small steamboat puffed by on the Mississippi. Passengers and crew caught the mood, and whistle and bell saluted; all cheered and waved hats and newspapers until the craft wheezed out of sight. But the sequel to this

---

[1] New Orleans *Daily Crescent*, January 29, 1861.
[2] Caskey, *Secession and Restoration of Louisiana*, 33.
[3] Pugh Plantation Diary, January 27, 1861.
[4] Ripley, *From Flag to Flag*, 10.

little affair pointed up the difference of opinion even within the same family, for when the master of Arlington—James McHatton, the delegate who had remained seated amidst the turmoil of the Charleston convention—returned to his plantation, he had his impulsive wife haul down the flag.[1]

The sands were fast running out for a South at peace, and cane planters were in the vanguard of militant Southerners. On February 7, 1861, Richard Taylor—sugar planter, son of a President of the United States, and future Confederate commander in Louisiana—introduced before the state convention a motion to create a state military organization.[2] Sugar growers used their influence to whip up zeal for the Southern cause. The Pughs in April distributed handbills calling a mass meeting of Bayou Lafourche folk "for the purpose of arousing a military spirit among [the] people." At the meeting on April 20 Richard Taylor delivered a fiery discourse against the "aggressor North."[3]

Planters lifted voices and pens to assert that there was no other course but to fight, since the prevailing sentiment was that without slavery the finest sugar plantation in the state would be worthless. They appealed to history with the argument: "The British thought our forefathers were wrong. We have ten times the cause for revolt which they had."[4] To them the elevation of a "Black Republican" to the presidency was an invasion of the sacred constitutional rights of the slave-owning South, an injustice to be righted only by resort to fire and sword.

In no expression from the sugar land, or from any other part of the South, for that matter, was there deeper venom than that of the oft-quoted prayer of the overseer of Magnolia Plantation below New Orleans: "This Day is set a part by presedent Jefferson Davis for fasting and praying owing to the Deplorable condishion ower Southern country is In My prayer Sincerely to God is that Every Black Republican in the Hole combined whorl Either man women o chile that is opposed to negro slavery as it existed in the Southern confederacy shal be trubled with pestilences & calamitys of all kinds & drag out the Balance of there existence in misry & degradation with Scarsely food & rayment enughf to keep sole & body to geather and O God I pray the to Direct

---

[1] *Ibid.*, 11-12.
[2] New Orleans *Daily Crescent*, February 7, 1861.
[3] Pugh Plantation Diary, April 18, 20, 1861.
[4] Caroline E. Merrick, *Old Times in Dixie Land; A Southern Matron's Memories* (New York, 1901), 28. Mrs. Merrick lived during the war on a cotton plantation located in an area where both cotton and sugar were grown.

a bullet or a bayonet to pirce the hart of every northern Soldier that invades southern Soil & after the Body has Rendered up its Traterish Sole gave it a trators reward a Birth in the Lake of fires & Brimstone My honest convicksion is that Every man women & chile that has gave aid to the abolishionist are fit Subjects for Hell I all so ask the to aide the Sothern confedercy in mantaining ower rites & establishing the confederate Government Believing in this case the prares from the wicked will prevailith much—Amen—." [1]

William Howard Russell found the faith of sugar planters in the Southern cause "indomitable." Their theory was that with trusted slaves to grow corn, sugar, and cotton, and with Southern youth to perform prodigies of valor on the battlefield, the Confederacy would be invincible. "With France and England to pour gold into their lap with which to purchase all they need in the contest, they believe they can beat all the powers of the Northern world in arms," wrote the famous journalist. Even the cane planters chanted the refrain, "Cotton is King," believing that the nations of Europe and their industries would be prostrate without the staple. [2] Also current was the opinion that without cotton and other Southern agricultural products the economy of the North would collapse. [3]

At this early stage the sugar planters' unquenchable faith in the military prowess of the South was matched by a high regard for the genius of President Jefferson Davis. A question invariably put to visitors from other parts was: "Have you seen our President, sir? don't you think him a very able man?" Russell felt that such unanimity in the estimate of the chief executive's character would itself prove of incalculable value in the impending struggle. [4] He failed to sense the quicksands of public opinion regarding the Confederate President.

With secession accomplished and war rapidly gathering head, bayou country planters threw their energy and means into the effort to raise troops for the cause, and parish police juries, dominated by sugar cultivators, hastened to vote funds for military purposes. In Iberville Parish $750 went to a militia unit, while organizations with colorful titles, like the Bayou Goula Guards, Iberville Grays, Home Sentinels,

---

[1] Magnolia Plantation Journal (1852-1862), June 13, 1861 (Microfilm copy in Southern Historical Collection, University of North Carolina Library, Chapel Hill).
[2] Russell, *My Diary North and South*, 260.
[3] *Ibid.*
[4] *Ibid.*

and Gros Tete Fencibles, received $500 each.[1] The Jefferson Parish police jury voted $1,000 to an elite cavalry unit known as the Jefferson Rangers,[2] and in St. Charles Parish $10,000 were appropriated to finance military companies and support families of volunteers.[3]

The town of Franklin on Bayou Teche was on April 23, 1861, the scene of the mustering of volunteers into a local military organization. Officers were selected, and the occasion gave opportunity for a number of distinguished citizens to display their patriotic rhetoric. Among the orators was Judge William T. Palfrey, well-known Bayou Teche sugar planter. The speakers seemed to compete with one another in tendering personal services and money to defend the flag of the Confederacy, drawing an editorial accolade to the effect that their "patriotism and gallantry had enshrined them in the heart of St. Mary [Parish]." After this outpouring of zeal the police jury found it easy to appropriate $20,000 for defense of parish and state.[4]

Many planters followed the example set by Palfrey in making personal contributions to the cause. John Hampden Randolph, one of the most prominent landowners of Iberville Parish, subscribed $500 to a $1,250,000 loan floated for defense of New Orleans, and gave $100 to the Bayou Goula Guards and varying amounts to other military formations in the parish.[5] Cane growers also made occasional donations for general relief of the needy in the emergency. On September 1, 1861, the Magnolia Plantation overseer scrawled with greater charity than literacy, "Shipt two Bals of Mollases and 282 Punkins to the Charity Markit [of New Orleans] for the Benefit of the Pore Per Str Empire Parish."[6]

In the closing months of 1861 and early 1862 many sugar growers and their sons joined the Confederate army. In St. John the Baptist

---

[1] Historical Records Survey, *Transcriptions of Parish Records of Louisiana; Number 24, Iberville Parish (Plaquemine)*, Series I, Police Jury Minutes (Baton Rouge, April, 1940-March, 1942), April 9, 1861. Hereinafter cited as *Iberville Parish Police Jury Minutes*.

[2] Historical Records Survey, *Transcriptions of Parish Records of Louisiana; Number 26, Jefferson Parish (Gretna)*, Series I, Police Jury Minutes (Baton Rouge, June, 1939-February, 1941), December 1, 1860. Hereinafter cited as *Jefferson Parish Police Jury Minutes*.

[3] St. Charles Parish Police Jury Minutes, September 24, 1861 (Transcription in the Department of Archives, Louisiana State University. Original in the St. Charles Parish courthouse, Hahnville, Louisiana).

[4] New Orleans *Daily Crescent*, April 23, 1861.

[5] Paul E. Postell, "John Hampden Randolph, A Southern Planter" (Unpublished M.A. Thesis, Louisiana State University, 1936), 118.

[6] Magnolia Plantation Journal, September 1, 1861.

Parish, for example, Captain Lezin Becnel organized a company called the Stephens Guards, which he led until he fell in action in Virginia.[1] A traveler chatted about military affairs with Alfred Roman, son of ex-Governor Andre Roman. This Creole planter's son commanded a company of men of the "best" families in the sugar country—"planters and the like".[2] The war spirit burned high among many of the folk of the sugar plantations.

Tragedy and gallantry came into the lives of sugar planters during the early, thrilling days of faraway war. The case of young Duncan Minor, son of William J. Minor, presented both. This seventeen-year-old lad joined the Natchez Light Infantry late in 1861 against the wishes of his father, who fumed that a "set of *foolish* women" had induced the boy to do so by playing upon his strong desire to serve his country. Early in 1862 Duncan Minor returned from Bowling Green, Kentucky, with typhoid fever, and the planter had a terrible premonition that his son would never leave the sickbed. On February 2 Minor implored the ministers of Natchez to pray for his failing son. Two weeks later the young soldier was dead, and the anguished parent wrote, "He deserved as much credit for patriotism as if he had been killed in battle."[3]

Plantation folk plunged with determination into the Civil War, and since the cane country lay far from the battle zone in Virginia and Kentucky, it appeared to be an unassailable base of manpower, money, and supplies for the Confederacy. A Baton Rouge volunteer rifle company contained nine planters and planters' sons out of a total of eighty-five members—a respectable number, since twenty-two occupations were represented in the organization.[4] The number of planter families who contributed without stint to the distant Southern armies is indeterminable. Certainly some of them opposed the conflict and did as little as possible to support it. But contemporary observers were agreed in the opinion that the people of the cane plantations as a rule gave generously of their sons and treasure to the cause of the Confederacy.

---

[1] Lubin F. Laurent, "History of St. John the Baptist Parish," *Louisiana Historical Quarterly*, VII (April, 1924), 325.

[2] Russell, *My Diary North and South*, 259.

[3] Minor Plantation Diary (1861-1862), c. 1862.

[4] William Watson, *Life in the Confederate Army; Being the Observations and Experiences of an Alien in the South during the American Civil War* (London, 1887), 126.

CHAPTER IV

EVE OF INVASION

The cane industry operated largely on borrowed capital; cultivators were prosperous as long as they enjoyed good credit. In normal times the New Orleans bankers and commission merchants provided a flexible source of money that enabled planters to draw funds for supplies throughout the year and make necessary adjustments when the crop was harvested and sent to market. Proprietors usually had little difficulty in renewing notes in case of unfavorable growing seasons, crevasses in the levee, or other unexpected mishaps.[1]

But 1860 was not a normal year. Anxiety in the business world mounted as political excitement heightened, and the economic stability of the sugar land soon was undermined. Cane producers were among the first to feel the general tightening of credit, a situation painfully reflected in a sudden decline in land value. New Orleans newspapers began to advertise sugar plantations at reduced prices, and in December A. Franklin Pugh attended an auction in which a place formerly worth $80,000 sold for almost one third less than that figure.[2]

The sensational events of secession absorbed much of the cane planters' time, and military preparations claimed their energies, but the humdrum activities of making sugar did not relax in face of these more thrilling affairs. A remarkable tenacity of routine continued through the tense days of 1860 and 1861, and on many places this discipline was never completely broken, even under the stringencies of invasion and military occupation. Sugar acreage planted in 1861 was high, since landowners based their crops on the amount of seed cane mattressed in the fall of 1860. The previous season had been good, yielding 228,753 hogsheads of sugar and 18,414,550 gallons of molasses. Rumblings of secession and war did not affect the 1861 acreage, for the cane was in the ground before the fighting began, and the next season's production was set except for the vagaries of the weather.[3]

---

[1] Prichard, "The Effects of the Civil War on the Louisiana Sugar Industry," *Journal of Southern History*, V (August, 1939), 319.
[2] Pugh Plantation Diary, December 27, 1860.
[3] Champomier, *Statement of the Sugar Crop Made in Louisiana in 1860-1861*, 39.

Nature favored the crop during the growing season of 1861. While masters talked politics and prepared for war, slaves went about routine chores with their customary indifference.[1] Operations on Magnolia Plantation were representative of affairs in the bayou land. After grinding ended in January of 1861 the overseer distributed boots and shoes to the Negroes. January, February, and part of March were occupied in planting seed cane and shipping sugar and molasses to New Orleans. By March 21 the planting was finished, with 425 arpents of cane in the furrows. While some of the slave gangs planted cane, others dropped corn, and by the end of the cane-planting period the overseer could report 104 arpents of corn in the ground.[2]

From the middle of March the Magnolia slaves were set to work cultivating cane, performing at the same time innumerable tasks subsidiary to sugar growing. In April additional corn was dropped. A group of Negroes went into the sugarhouse to clean and repair machinery. Fence building occupied the time of others. The overseer dispatched one gang to hoe ratoons and two days later ordered nine two-mule plows into the ratoons for the purpose of "baring them off," while eighteen plows were sent into the plant cane.[3]

The fateful events at Fort Sumter on April 12 had no effect on the persistence of routine on Magnolia Plantation. Throughout the remainder of the month the slave force was divided into hoe gangs and plow gangs. On April 26 while one gang hoed, twenty-three plows worked plant cane, and at the same time four-mule plows broke ground for additional planting. On April 29 a corn crusher began operations, and during the following weeks numerous references to its use appeared in the plantation journal. May was devoted almost exclusively to plowing and hoeing the developing cane shoots. On May 29 the dread stock disease, charbon, appeared and killed a mule. In June the Magnolia blacks enjoyed a dubious respite from cane cultivation when the overseer put all hands to setting sweet potato slips. Attention to auxiliary crops took up the remainder of the month.[4]

In July the Magnolia Plantation labor force began to make prepara-

---

[1] Champomier, *Statement of the Sugar Crop Made in Louisiana in 1861-1862*, vii-viii.

[2] Magnolia Plantation Journal, January 20, March 21, 1861. An arpent is about four fifths of an acre.

[3] *Ibid.*, April 8, 1861. Ratoons are shoots from cane cut in previous seasons, which if permitted to mature produce sugar, though not as heavily as plant cane. "Baring off" is plowing the earth away from the cane.

[4] *Ibid.*, April 26, 29, June 10, 1861.

tions to receive the harvest. A number of workers were selected from plow and hoe gangs and ordered to split hoop poles. Plantation coopers were busy shaving staves and building hogsheads and barrels. Charbon in the meantime ravaged the livestock unabated, and by the end of the month twenty-five out of ninety mules were dead of it.[1] By August the crop was approaching maturity and required little attention; all hands were in full preparation for the cutting season. Throughout the month the cutting of wood for boilers, ditch cleaning, hogshead making, fodder pulling, and road mending went on unimpeded. An entry chosen at random from the overseer's journal presented this diversity of tasks: "18 men Ditching, 34 In Corn Crib till noon, After noon cleaning Ditches, 7 men shaving Staves, 2 men at Draning Mashean, 4 men working on mud Boat, 4 in Hospital."[2] Political disturbances had little effect in 1861 on the life and labor of Magnolia Plantation slaves.

The Negroes began cutting cane on October 14, with thirty-one knives working and eight carts hauling cane to the sugarhouse. Women with suckling babies scrubbed the sugarhouse in anticipation of hectic weeks of grinding ahead. Once grinding was under way it proceeded at mad pace, for planters soon knew that the yield would be great. The large amount of seed cane planted the previous winter, coupled with an unusually favorable growing season, had paved the way for a record-breaking crop. Magnolia Plantation slaves were assigned as follows: "19 hauling cane, 40 cutting, 11 readying cane for the mill, 2 preparing hogsheads, 20 working sugar house machinery, 8 working in stables, 11 working in dwelling house, 1 working in the garden, 2 unloading coal at the wharf, 3 nursing, 17 sick."[3]

On many places slaves labored on Christmas Day in the heavy 1861-1862 harvest. The Bayside Plantation Journal entry—"Christmas day, all hard at work making sugar"—told the story. When returns were in, most individual plantations reflected the general prosperity of the season. On February 3, 1862, the Magnolia Plantation sugarhouse closed down after having turned out 1,800 hogsheads of sugar, and the owner later wrote with a surge of pride: "Began to Roll 15 Ocbr—1861 Made 1800 Hds Sugar on Magnolia Plantation Largest Crop ever made on one place with 80 hands."[4] The total crop of the state was 459,410 hogsheads

---

[1] *Ibid.*, August 12, 1861.
[2] *Ibid.*
[3] *Ibid.*, November 17, 1861.
[4] *Ibid.*, February 3, 1862.

—the greatest in the history of the industry to that time.[1]

Most sugar plantations strove for self-sufficiency before the war. Legend has it that Valcour Aime of St. James Parish once won a $10,000 wager by serving a perfect dinner, all of which—fish, game, fruits, nuts, coffee, cigars, and wine—he supplied from his estate.[2] Not every planter, however, was a Valcour Aime, and few places on the eve of war were able to maintain themselves in basic foodstuffs. Magnolia Plantation purchased in 1860 large quantities of rice, corn, flour, bran, straw, hay, peas, beef, pork, and fish, and these shortages were not overcome during the war.[3] Other plantations were in the same predicament. In February of 1861 William T. Palfrey of St. Mary Parish intercepted a flatboat of corn on Bayou Teche and bought 500 barrels.[4] During the same month Governor Thomas O. Moore, a Rapides Parish sugar planter, procured $210 worth of pork for his slaves.[5] Judge John Moore of St. Mary Parish made numerous purchases of pork during the winter.[6]

Bayou country inhabitants were aware of this shortage and of the danger it entailed in case of war. As early as January of 1861 citizens began to urge a shift in agriculture from sugar to corn. One writer, adopting the fitting pen name, Agricola, felt that sufficient land should be planted in corn to feed the entire South, and that this should be done even if the season were unfavorable. "If our people have enough to eat," he opined, "they can defy the world in arms—Forewarned—forearmed!"[7] William Howard Russell found that Louisiana sugar planters at least partially heeded this admonition, that they had put an exceptional amount of land into corn in the spring of 1861.[8]

Sugar planters at first failed to grasp the significance to their industry of naval and economic warfare. Russell was interested upon learning that a favorite theme of conversation among them held that it was

---

[1] Champomier, *Statement of the Sugar Crop Made in Louisiana in 1861-1862*, 39.

[2] Work Projects Administration, *Louisiana; a Guide to the State*, 553.

[3] For a list of these purchases see J. Carlyle Sitterson, "Magnolia Plantation, 1852-1862; a Decade of a Louisiana Sugar Estate," *Mississippi Valley Historical Review* (Cedar Rapids), XXV (September, 1938), 204-205.

[4] Palfrey Plantation Diary, February 2, 1861.

[5] Invoice from A. Miltenberger to Thomas O. Moore, February 1, 1861, Thomas O. Moore Papers (Department of Archives, Louisiana State University).

[6] John Moore Plantation Journal (1847-1867), January 3, 1861 (Department of Archives, Louisiana State University).

[7] New Orleans *Daily Crescent*, January 18, 1861.

[8] Russell, *My Diary North and South*, 265.

absurd to suppose that they could be injured by blockade. This correspondent—a navy-conscious Englishman—soberly warned, "They may find out, however, that [a blockade] is no contemptible means of warfare." Planter John Burnside of Ascension Parish did not share the optimism of most cane producers and was apprehensive about his prospects because of the war. He had expected to realize in the neighborhood of $400,000 from his immense crop; he now stood instead to lose heavily if sugar could not be shipped to the North. "I fancy, indeed," asserted Russell, "he more and more regrets that he embarked his capital in these great sugarswamps, and that he would gladly invest it at a loss in the old country [Ireland]." [1]

Soon the Federal navy controlled the Gulf of Mexico, clamping the great Mississippi River trade artery and cutting off sugar cultivators from their markets. The price of sugar sank as that of corn, pork, and other plantation necessities climbed. The problem of feeding and clothing slaves quickly became urgent to Louisiana planters. A. Franklin Pugh analyzed the situation glumly after a visit to New Orleans in October of 1861: "[There were] more people than I ever before saw at this season. Everything is very high and looking upwards except sugar and molasses which are both going down very rapidly.... I doubt if 50 hhds of New Sugar and 200 Bbs of New Molasses have been received and yet the market has fallen from 9 cts to 6 cts [a pound] since the first was sold." [2]

War made itself felt early on sugar plantations by sweeping away much of the white manpower of lower Louisiana. The South had always boasted of her ability to supply armies with white sons while faithful slaves tended the fields. She was now put to the test. This deficiency did not harm plantations as much as it did small farms, but it nevertheless dealt them a serious blow. The planters' ingenuity was severely taxed to replace personnel who left early for service. Slaves took the places of skilled white artisans and ditch diggers on most places, but the overseer shortage was more critical. This problem usually was solved by the simple expedient of doing without, and many owners out of patriotism doubled up in managing plantations during the emergency. [3]

Louisiana sugar planters formed a pro-tariff minority in the midst of the anti-tariff cotton growers. Observers were quick to spot the

---

[1] *Ibid.*, 265, 283.
[2] Pugh Plantation Diary, October 12, 1861.
[3] For a discussion of this problem see Bell I. Wiley, *Southern Negroes, 1861-1865* (New Haven, 1938), 50.

anomaly of a situation in which a group whose livelihood depended upon protection cast its lot with the offspring of nullificationists. The Louisville *Journal* in February of 1861 chided sugar proprietors for their role in secession, predicting that the Confederacy would lower or abolish the duty on sugar. "And how do you think your sugar planters will relish the change?" taunted the Kentucky journalist. "Won't they be as sour as their sugar is sweet?" [1] The editor of the New Orleans *Daily Crescent* took up the literary challenge, replying that no one knew what would be the tariff policy under the Confederacy. He retorted smugly that Louisiana planters had loftier aims than sheer monetary gain. "Perhaps they will be still more astonished," he stated, "when we tell them that a majority of the sugar parishes of the State elected delegates to the convention, in favor of immediate secession." [2]

Cane growers obviously hoped for tariff concessions from their cotton-producing political bedmates. William J. Minor summarized the attitude of his class when he wrote: "The friends of the Hon D. F. Kenner will bring him out as a candidate for the Senate of the C. S.— I think, he is the man for the times & the place, & especially the man to represent the sugar interest—Howell Cobb told me Kenner made more reputation in the provisional congress than an[y] man in it—If we can elect Kenner to the Senate, we will beat the jew Benjamin, who, I understand will be a candidate, & will enable us to Send an other good *sugar* man to the lower house." [3] From these references to the sugar interest, one can surmise that the planters of lower Louisiana expected to regain in the Confederacy old favors enjoyed under the Union.

The parishes of the sugar country were in the heart of the slave region, and the question of the Negroes' behavior was vital to all citizens. Southerners traditionally contended that the blacks were so well-treated and happy that they could not be induced to revolt. Facing the crisis of war, they were not so sure. The election of a "Black Republican" to the presidency and the rumbling of war chariots in the distance caused them to look fearfully upon the throngs of Negroes about them who could at the right moment burst into rebellion.

Patrols were always a part of the discipline of Southern Negroes, but in many cases these organizations existed on the statute books only,

---

[1] New Orleans *Daily Crescent*, February 6, 1861.
[2] *Ibid.*
[3] William J. Minor to T. J. Wells, November 19, 1861, William J. Minor and Family Papers (Department of Archives, Louisiana State University).

and except for moments of alarm, whites were perfunctory in carrying out assigned duties. Planters of lower Louisiana set about late in 1860 to close up the gaps in their system of control. The section's unenforced patrol policy was reshaped in order to assure that the slaves would remain docile in the midst of rapidly mounting tension regarding their future.

Patrol regulations adopted by the St. Charles Parish police jury were a good example of measures designed to curb the activities of the Negroes in the cane land. The parish was split into five districts, each with a patrol and patrol chief. Patrols were to make rounds twice a week for at least six hours at a time, and were charged to be particularly alert on Saturday nights and on the eve of feasts and gatherings. All white men between eighteen and fifty were eligible to serve and must do so at appointed times. In case of a disturbance involving Negroes, the patrol chief was to deputize all white men in his district. Patrols had authority, with permission of owners or overseers, to make inspections of slave quarters, and any strange Negro discovered without a pass was to receive twenty lashes and be placed in stocks until his owner arrived to claim him. Whites were forbidden to trade with Negroes. All plantations were to have at least one white person present per thirty blacks. Slaves could not bear arms of any sort off the plantation, and owners who permitted Negroes to hunt must confine them to the immediate premises and provide them with written permits to the effect that they were hunting.[1]

In February of 1861 David Pugh of Madewood Plantation on the Lafourche observed that the Negroes of that area had in mind that they were to be set free on the fourth of March, and he proposed a patrol in Assumption Parish to let them know the error of their way. Patrols soon were riding the countryside in this parish, and the Pughs were active in them. The group of which A. Franklin Pugh was a member met once a week at Florian Rodrigue's store to plan activities of the coming week. At a meeting on July 21 the men decided to set up a special patrol to circulate once a week after midnight, in addition to the regular patrols already in operation.[2]

War hysteria quickened in the cane land, and with it came suppression of the civil liberties of suspicious white citizens. In December of 1860 a vigilance committee formed in Lafourche Parish and drove off an objectionable white man. A. Franklin Pugh felt that the action had a

---

[1] St. Charles Parish Police Jury Minutes, December 19, 1860.
[2] Pugh Plantation Diary, February 24, July 21, 1861.

very happy effect on the behavior of the Negro population of the neighborhood and opined that such a committee "would do good in Assumption [Parish]."[1] Unofficial police action always sows the seeds of anarchy, and there were unwarranted acts of violence in the bayou country. In May of 1861 Pugh saw the danger as he recorded that a group had "killed a poor harmless man in Paincourtville... A very cowardly act—."[2]

As the summer of 1861 wore on, citizens of lower Louisiana grew increasingly apprehensive of the Negroes, and this fear showed instantly in a tightening of the shackles. The Iberville Parish police jury in June decreed that no slave could own a boat or skiff. Those found with boats in their possession were to receive fifteen lashes. White men were to accompany groups of slaves moving from one plantation to another. No Negro was allowed to marry on a neighboring plantation without the written consent of both masters, and in cases where slaves were married to women on other places—"broad wives" in the parlance of the quarter—husbands were permitted to visit but twice a week. When visits were made, the blacks had to bear passes explaining their marital situations and specifying visiting nights.[3]

Most patrols apparently were conducted with a fair degree of discipline and restraint. Patrol captains frequently were planters, men who had an interest in the welfare and just treatment of Negroes. But an incident that occurred in St. Mary Parish proved that this was not universally true and demonstrated the savagery to which Negroes sometimes were subjected at the sadistic whim of the whites. William T. Palfrey wrote in hot indignation: "Last night, about 9 o'clock a Mr. Whittaker overseer for Mr. Bethell and an engineer at work for Mr. Lynch, beat in a cruel manner, one of Mrs. Meades' Negro men (Abram) on his way to my plantation, and in my lane—also took into custody my negro man Little Edward, without provocation & on my premises.—Also the mulatto man—Henry, belonging to Mr. Meade, & took all three to Mr. B's town place—I followed & found all three in the stocks, the negro Abram covered with his own blood, his clothes torn from him, & beaten & swollen in a terrible manner. I procured the release of Henry and Edward, but the release of Abram was refused on the ground that he had resisted—He said he had only struggled to get away, thinking

---

[1] *Ibid.*, December 14, 1860.
[2] *Ibid.*, May 30, 1861.
[3] *Iberville Parish Police Jury Minutes*, June 4, 1861.

they meant to kill him.—It was a brutal transaction on the part of these men, as I believe—having known Abram for the last 15 years, as a harmless, inoffensive negro.—Has a wife & family on my plantation, & was as usual, coming to visit them. Being employed at the time at his mistress' place which adjoins my own, he thought, as he told them, that for so short a distance, he did not need a pass.—These men were not patrolling but returning from Centreville, & no doubt intoxicated when Abram was beaten, was about 100 yds. below my sugar house gates—They stopped & abducted Henry & Edward about 100 yds, within my lower line, passing as they went, by Mrs. Meade's gate."[1]

Analysis of this sorry episode casts light on race and class relations in the cane country during those taut days. The beating was not done nor was it approved by a planter; Overseer Whittaker exhibited the hostility that whites of his class so often felt for the Negro. Whittaker's employer, P. C. Bethell—as Palfrey explained in a marginal note in his diary—was absent at the time and thus was unable to stay his subordinate's vicious hand. The white men involved were not on an authorized patrol, which probably would have been commanded by some responsible citizen—perhaps a planter—and would have been conducted soberly. If Abram had been intercepted by a patrol, he doubtless would have been given a specified number of lashes and held under arrest until his mistress claimed him, but would have escaped the bludgeoning of these drunken whites. Palfrey's account of the incident also revealed a disregard on his part for the strict letter of the law where Negroes were concerned, since obviously he saw nothing wrong in Abram's visiting his wife without a pass, though police jury regulations required one. This was perhaps characteristic of the great planters' tendency to temper the stringencies of patrol rules with common sense.

The overseer's refusal to surrender Abram to a man of Palfrey's reputation raises an interesting point. Why would a lower-class white defy the wishes of a wealthy judge and sugar planter? It can be assumed that Whittaker took advantage in this affair of the rising hostility against and fear of the Negro brought on by the nature of the times.

Levee patrols were vital to planters of lower Louisiana, for a crevasse in the Mississippi dike could quickly undo the wealthiest proprietor. Plantation families often were haunted by this specter. "It is a fearful sight," declared one inhabitant, "to see the relentless flood plunging

---

[1] Palfrey Plantation Diary, June 9, 1861.

by,... many feet above the ground on which you stand, an embankment of earth your only defense, and the waves of passing steamboats.... falling in spray at your feet." [1] Since one cut of a spade possibly could create a fissure in the levee, it usually was watched day and night by "trusty men with shovels and lanterns," who guarded against the occurrence of such a calamity. By 1862, however, fear of the Negroes outstripped that of crevasses. When a levee inspector discovered a dangerously weak spot near Baton Rouge and notified all planters in the vicinity, they failed to respond. So fearful were they of permitting their slaves to assemble, "so apprehensive lest they communicate from plantation to plantation, and a stray spark enkindle the fires of sedition and rebellion," that they withheld the Negroes and permitted the leak to go unattended. As a result, the river bored a great hole in the levee below the capital city and ruined the cane fields for miles about. [2]

Effective patrol activity contributed greatly to the decorum of Negroes during the early months of war. No untoward incidents occurred among the blacks before the arrival of the Federal army. The state legislature was cognizant of the importance of this form of slave discipline, and in 1862 passed an act subjecting to a fine of ten dollars or twenty-four hours' imprisonment any eligible citizen who failed to take his assigned place on patrol. [3]

Social life in the sugar parishes felt the effects of secession and war, as within a few months after Fort Sumter most of the young men were gone from the plantations. This sweeping away of boys—sons of planters and brothers and beaux of plantation daughters—inevitably altered the colorful entertainments of the section. The departure of planters and their sons to the army gave occasion for varied social activities. Some left with the music of plantation dances ringing in their ears, while to others, departure was marked by a blend of patriotism and religion. When Captain Lezin Becnel of St. John the Baptist Parish gathered his Stephens Guards together to leave for the fighting zone, he marched the organization into the Church of St. John the Baptist, and there in solemn and formal ceremony received his flag. The large standard presented to Captain Becnel was made by the patriotic women of the parish and was thus a cherished emblem to the young soldiers. The commander then led his formation out of the church and down to the

---

[1] Ripley, *From Flag to Flag*, 19.
[2] *Ibid.*, 20.
[3] Wiley, *Southern Negroes, 1861-1865*, 34.

river, where lay the steamboat *Mississippi*. The steamer moved off to the noise of wild cheering on shore as a band broke into the stirring thunder of the *Marseillaise*, and Captain Lezin Becnel—Creole sugar planter and Confederate officer—looked upon the cane fields for the last time. He fell in battle in Virginia.[1]

Temporary encampments sprang up in parts of the cane land, imparting a brief fever flash of excitement to the social life of nearby plantations. Young officers in handsome uniforms came to the planters' homes for dinners and parties, while wives, sisters, and sweethearts "virtually lived" in the camps. "Spotless new tents, with bright flags flying, the young men thronging around the carriages which brought their mothers and sisters as daily visitors" left ineffaceable memories with the inhabitants of the sugar land.[2]

Weddings remained high lights in the social affairs of plantation folk. A. Franklin Pugh and his family in April of 1861 attended the marriage ceremony of R. C. Martin, Jr., and Maggie Littlejohn at Melrose Plantation, the Littlejohn estate on Bayou Lafourche. The evidence of war was conspicuous in the absence of many friends of by-gone days, in spite of which Pugh felt that the affair went off most pleasantly. Political and military cares apparently were abandoned. Dinner ended at about two-thirty in the afternoon, after which all guests remained in lively conversation until about dark.[3]

Planters and friends who were still at home continued to hunt and fish as their sons left for the battle area. A group of hunters in August of 1861 chased a deer into the fields of Boatner Plantation on the Lafourche, but their marksmanship was faulty. In March of the next year the Pugh family engaged in an adventure doubtless borrowed from the plantation Negroes; they took off on a crawfishing expedition.[4] On the very eve of Federal invasion the Pughs remained fishermen, for the entire family journeyed in April to Bayou Corn to take part in a fishing frolic along with other planter families.[5]

Confederate appeal to God for victory on the battlefield lent a religious overtone to some of the activities of sugar plantation folk. President Jefferson Davis in November of 1861 declared a fast day throughout

---

[1] Laurent, "History of St. John the Baptist Parish," *Louisiana Historical Quarterly*, VII (April, 1924), 325.
[2] Merrick, *Old Times in Dixie Land*, 87.
[3] Pugh Plantation Diary, April 25, 1861.
[4] *Ibid.*, March 1, 1862.
[5] *Ibid.*, April 11, 1862.

the South, and citizens of the cane land gathered into their churches to offer prayers for sons in the field. William T. Palfrey suspended all work on his place, though he was in the heat of grinding, and he and his family went to church and fasted throughout the day.[1] With sons facing death in far-off Virginia, sugar planters drew nearer to God for solace and assurance.

Churchgoing was traditionally a gay event to proprietors and their families, and even under the gravity of the times these assemblages continued to afford excellent opportunity for the airing of news and gossip. The chief effect of the war in its early stages was the shortage of young men. Although A. Franklin Pugh was not regular in church attendance, his family was reasonably faithful. His diary throughout 1861 was punctuated with entries such as: "... Miss Duval [a guest]... went to the Catholic church, and Henry and Bell ... went to the Methodist Church. Rev. Mr. Davis took dinner with us today—."[2]

Most social events during the war had a military flavor, since frequently the object of citizens of lower Louisiana was to combine entertainment with promotion of the Confederate cause. Bayou country women staged "every species of bazaar, supper, candy-pulling and tableaux that would raise a dollar for the army."[3] Plantation wives near Baton Rouge joined city women in organizing a "Campaign Sewing Society" whose primary purpose was to make uniforms and knit stockings for the Southern army. The very name of the group suggested how transient the members considered the emergency. A prominent lady in the organization took great pride in the fact that she advanced to the point that she could, by knitting at every available moment, turn out one short cotton stocking a day.

The society met regularly to discuss plans for raising money for the Confederacy, and out of these conferences arose the idea of holding a "tombola"—a great lottery where all the prizes were donated, and every ticket drew a prize. Tickets sold for one dollar each. The energetic women secured a large hall, a stable, and a warehouse in which to store contributions. An amazing variety of gifts accumulated, and the colorful event came off in the following manner: "The hall soon was overflowing with minor articles from houses and shops. Nothing either was too costly or too insignificant to be refused. A glass showcase glittered with jewelry

---

[1] Palfrey Plantation Diary, November 15, 1861.
[2] Pugh Plantation Diary, May 26, 1861.
[3] Merrick, *Old Times in Dixie Land*, 54.

of all styles and patterns, and bits of rare old silver. Pictures and engravings, old and faded, new and valuable, hung side by side on the walls. Odd pieces of furniture, work-boxes, lamps and candelabra, were arranged here and there, to stand out in bold relief amid an immense array of pencils, tweezers, scissors, penknives, tooth-picks, darning-needles, and such trifles. The stalls of the stable were tenanted by mules, cows, hogs, with whole litters of pigs, and varieties of poultry. The warehouse groaned under the weight of barrels of sugar, molasses, and rice, and bushels of meal, potatoes, turnips, and corn. As is ever the case, the blind goddess was capricious: with the exception of an old negro woman, who won a set of pearls, I can not remember any one who secured a prize worth the price of the ticket. I invested in twenty tickets, for which I received nineteen leadpencils and a frolicsome old goat, with beard hanging to his knees...." [1]

The tombola was for the moment an overwhelming success. The women who sponsored it spent nothing and made a profit of $6,000. But fate and the Union navy were unkind to these patriotic ladies of the sugar land, for before the proceeds could be sent to New Orleans, the city had fallen to the Yankees. Cut off from supplies and with all communications severed, the society disbanded. "The busy workers," recalled a member, "retired to their houses, the treasurer fled with the funds for safe-keeping, and, when she emerged from her retreat, six thousand dollars in Confederate paper was not worth six cents." [2]

Plantation women of Assumption Parish met at the home of A. Franklin Pugh and worked out a plan for making uniforms for the parish volunteers. Pugh felt that they had a system that would be successful, in which the men would provide cloth for the undertaking, while the women were to do the sewing. [3] Public recitals and concerts also were staged to raise funds. In August of 1861 the Pugh family attended a concert in Napoleonville, given to raise money to purchase woolen shirts for volunteers. Shortly afterward another concert was put on for the benefit of a blind music teacher who had given his services freely in raising money for the soldiers. [4]

The stress of political and military affairs failed to dampen the sugar planters' love of good horseflesh. William J. Minor ended a letter of

---

[1] Ripley, *From Flag to Flag*, 13-15.
[2] *Ibid.*, 16.
[3] Pugh Plantation Diary, July 9, 1861.
[4] *Ibid.*, October 10, 1861.

November 18, 1861, that was primarily concerned with political matters, with a note that he had six horses in training, all doing well.[1] Only a few days before Federal troops swept across this proprietor's Terrebonne Parish plantations, he appeared more interested in watching his fine horses run than in the ominous face of the future.[2]

As cane planters eagerly awaited news from battles in Virginia during the early months of conflict, many smaller social events continued undisturbed. Dinners remained a favorite form of polite intercourse; William Howard Russell dined sumptuously with a group of the most affluent proprietors in the state, including John Burnside, Duncan Kenner, and M. S. Bringier.[3] The A. Franklin Pughs were favored with frequent visits by their acquaintances, usually ladies, who came to dine and spend the night at Boatner Plantation on the Lafourche. Distant war changed but did not crush the rich social life of the bayou land.

Patrols rode the countryside through the dark watches of the night, restricting the movements of the Negroes, but slaves were not denied all social activities. William J. Minor in 1861 gave his hands on Waterloo Plantation two days off for Christmas and donated a hog, a barrel of flour, and one fourth of a barrel of sugar for a great dinner. After dinner the Negroes were to have a ball in the sugarhouse, and the cautious master noted, "Strict decorum must be preserved at the Ball—No one must wear a hat in the room...."[4] Nor did William T. Palfrey allow the heavy sugar harvest to interfere with his workers' holidays, for he jotted into his diary on December 25, "Christmas—holidays commenced—," and on January 2, 1862, "Holidays ended—work begun—."[5]

Life, labor, and diversion continued in the cane land on the eve of invasion, for the tenacity of routine on sugar plantations remained unshaken. Masters found their days fuller than ever before, with patrol duties often added to those of running the cane establishments. They frequently were obliged to take on tasks ordinarily performed by overseers, as these subordinates left for the fighting fronts. Slaves went their

---

[1] William J. Minor to T. J. Wells, November 19, 1861, William J. Minor and Family Papers.
[2] Minor Plantation Diary (1861-1862), April 1, 1862.
[3] Russell, *My Diary North and South*, 279.
[4] Minor Plantation Diary (1861-1865), December 19, 20, 1861.
[5] Palfrey Plantation Diary, December 25, 1861, January 2, 1862.

plodding ways, but were not as oblivious of events in the offing as their patient faces indicated. Sensing an undercurrent of malaise, planters renovated obsolete control machinery and forbade the assembly of more than a handful of laborers. Social life flagged in many areas as war robbed plantations of their sons, but in others near Confederate encampments the tempo rose, and the sugar country was charged with mounting tension as the realization grew that the land was at war.

CHAPTER V

BLOCKADE AND INVASION

Louisiana felt secure from invasion by land, for she was located behind a tier of states that spread from Virginia to Arkansas and constituted the stout buckler of the Confederacy. These border states absorbed the thrusts of the Union army for many months, sheltering the lower South from assault. Louisiana's peril in war lay in what had been her blessing in peace—her position on the Gulf of Mexico and the great Mississippi River system. The lower parishes were traversed by four waterways capable of introducing hostile naval craft into the interior of the state. These were the Mississippi River, the Atchafalaya River, Bayou Lafourche, and Bayou Teche. The southern region of Louisiana —the cane country—was the soft underbelly of the Confederacy.

Federal military authorities were not unaware of the vulnerability of the Gulf area. In June of 1861 a Northern blockade became effective off the mouth of the Mississippi, and shortly the other outlets were clamped. The cogency of William Howard Russell's warning as to the danger of a blockade now came to the sugar growers in a crystal flash of realization, for the strangling effects of naval power soon were apparent. In the fall of 1861 producers faced the problem of disposing of their crop; by November the grinding season was well under way, and owners were aware that they would have an extraordinarily heavy yield.

Planters usually marketed produce in one of three ways. Most of them shipped it down the Mississippi to commission merchants in New Orleans, where the sugar was sold to the highest bidder at the levee market. Others preferred to sell on the plantation wharves to merchants from St. Louis, Cincinnati, and the Eastern cities. Still others sold their merchandise in the sugarhouses, in which case purchasers removed sugar and molasses at their own expense and responsibility.[1]

The misfortune of having to depend upon an inadequate transportation system joined the woes inflicted by the blockade in choking off the sugar market in the fall of 1861. Under normal conditions, planters could have distributed much of their produce throughout the hinterland by rail.

---

[1] Walter Prichard, "A Louisiana Sugar Plantation under the Slavery Regime," *Mississippi Valley Historical Review*, XIV (September, 1927), 177.

Unfortunately the Confederate railway system was taxed beyond capacity in moving troops and supplies to threatened areas in Virginia and Kentucky. A great planter from below New Orleans caught the full significance of the plight: "While Magnolias sugar Sold at 10 4 [10.4 cents per pound] So far—but market Dull—owing to impossibility of Shipping it—Poor Sugars are hardly worth anything — $1\frac{1}{2}$ to $2\frac{1}{4}$ — for Refining grades—I fear we shall not be able to do anything with our Sugars—As there is no way of Distributing them throu the Country—The Blockade & the Railroads all rushed with carrying Troops and Supplies—." [1]

The other edge of the sword of blockade was just as sharp, for not only were planters severed from their markets, they also were cut off from sources of supply. Prices of plantation necessities soared, and a landowner recorded: "Pork 45.$ per Bl Bacon 25 ... Salt $10. per Sack—Beef Cattle 2 to 3 Prices and few to be had and every thing wanted for Supplies in Shape of Necessaries Very Scarce and very High Fabulous Prices." [2] The same cultivator noted a few days later that the railroads at Memphis and Grand Junction, Tennessee, were terribly congested, and that his white sugar, which up to that time had been in great demand, could no longer be sold at any price. "I fear," he commented soberly, "that we Shall not be able to Ship or Sell any more Sugars for Some time as all the Transportation is taken up on the Rail Roads by our Troops and their Supplies." On the eve of invasion New Orleans commission merchants sent out the grim word that the market was dull and slow, with sugar "very irregular." [3]

Only one solution to the problem of blockade was possible. Sugar producers would have to discover ways of shipping to new markets within the Confederacy, and during the latter part of the grinding season of 1862 the more resourceful proprietors began to work toward that end. Demand for sugar and molasses was great, for the South needed this produce perhaps more urgently than ever before. The effects of the blockade and the severing of ties with the Northwest left Southern slave owners wanting cheap food for their wards, and in desperation they turned to molasses as a substitute, with the result that the consumption

---

[1] Magnolia Plantation Journal, November 3, 1861.
[2] *Ibid.*, November 8, 1861.
[3] Darby and Fremantle to John Moore, April 19, 1862, David Weeks and Family Papers (Department of Archives, Louisiana State University).

of this by-product vastly increased throughout the South during 1862.[1]

Cotton planters looked to sugar growers for assistance in feeding their slaves. As early as October of 1861 the owner of a Bayou Lafourche plantation received a letter requesting sugar and molasses. The writer's salutation and opening sentence indicated an overnight renewal of an old friendship under the exigencies of the times. "My dear Charley," began this quondam friend, "You will no doubt be somewhat surprised at receiving a letter from me as it has been several years since I have written to you." Then to the point, "As there is great scarcity of meat in the country, every planter I believe is trying to get a good supply of molasses." He would be happy to exchange bales of cotton, at a fair price, for eight or nine barrels of molasses and a barrel of good sugar. He went on to say that he had been trading cotton for salt, Negroes' shoes, and other items, and that he hoped the cane planter would look with favor upon a similar arrangement.[2]

Different plans were advanced for buying sugar and molasses, most of them involving no cash. On October 29 a cotton planter opened a letter of request in a manner perhaps designed to be peculiarly effective in the South, adopting a kinsfolk approach—"Dear Cousin Charles"—in the salutation. This writer also desired sugar and molasses, for which he proposed to make a note payable sixty days after the lifting of the blockade. Doubtless relying upon his kinship to obtain special favors, he was fussy as to the type of molasses and arrangements for shipping. "Please send me a choice article," he implored. "For molasses will be my main dependence to feed my negroes." He also wished twenty or twenty-five barrels for his mother, but with sublime filial disregard he urged that his own produce be sent first. Pushing his parsimony to the limit, he requested that the sugar be shipped on either the *Lafourche* or the *Natchez*, since he felt that the captains of these steamboats would "wait a little while for their freight bill." In the margin of this letter the sender reiterated his plea that the sugar and molasses be sent as soon as possible, bringing his insistent message to a close with another not-too-subtle reminder of family ties, "Your affectionate cousin."[3]

Cotton planters sometimes failed to appreciate the trials of their

---

[1] Wiley, *Southern Negroes, 1861-1865*, 27.

[2] M. Buck to Charles Mathews, October 9, 1861, Charles Mathews and Family Papers.

[3] W. H. Buck to Charles Mathews, October 29, 1861, Charles Mathews and Family Papers.

sugar-growing brethren and often looked with envy upon their lot. An Alabama planter wrote in December of 1861 that he had no money, that his slaves soon would be out of meat, and that he did not know how to feed them except on molasses, bread, and a little beef. Then came an entreaty to a sugar cultivator for thirty or forty barrels of molasses, payable when the war ended. The planter closed with this invidious shot: "If the war continues you Sugar planters will get very rich. Sugar & molasses will be very high. Molasses now in Mobile at 45 cts per gall."[1] The pastures of the sugar industry looked much greener from a distance than they did to the men who owned them.

Cane producers sought to market their crop throughout the entire South, but the congestion of the railroads usually forced them to ship to cities and plantations on or near rivers and accessible to steamboats. Many landowners looked to Texas as an outlet for their blockaded wares. In January of 1862 a St. Mary Parish cultivator outlined plans to visit Houston in an effort to find buyers. He purchased a boat and shipped a quantity of sugar to the Texas community.[2] Beaumont, Texas, also provided an outlet for a small amount of Louisiana sugar during the winter of 1862.[3]

Some planters held off in their search for inland markets in the belief that the blockade, and even the war, would be brief. The fall of New Orleans in April of 1862 abruptly dispelled these illusions. After the invasion cane growers began a frantic effort to dispose of the huge stocks in their sugarhouses. In May a prominent planter on Bayou Teche began to send produce up the Red River to Jefferson, Texas, while other consignments went up the Ouachita River into north Louisiana and Arkansas. The Bayou Teche producer pointed out that Camden, Arkansas, was a likely market, and that he had discovered a boatman who would haul sugar there for considerably less than the prevailing charge for shipping to Texas.[4]

The often haphazard methods of marketing sugar under wartime handicaps reflected the desperation of the planters' search for buyers. In May a proprietor revealed that he was shipping sugar on a steamboat

---

[1] Sam Mathews to Charles Mathews, December 8, 1861, Charles Mathews and Family Papers.
[2] A. C. Weeks to John Moore, January 13, 1862, David Weeks and Family Papers.
[3] Receipt from Southern Mutual Insurance Company to John Moore, May 31, 1862, David Weeks and Family Papers.
[4] L. W. Moore to John Moore, May 14, 1862, David Weeks and Family Papers.

bound for Jefferson, Texas, and that since he knew no purchasers there, he was turning his wares over to the captain of the vessel, who was to dispose of them at the best price he could obtain. The planter requested a friend in Shreveport to assist the boatman in this effort. "Not being acquainted with any person there in whom confidence may be placed to Sell the Sugar," he wrote plaintively, "I have to beg of you to recommend [the captain of the boat] to some person." [1]

In May of 1862 William T. Palfrey of St. Mary Parish shipped fifteen hogsheads of sugar on the steamer *Little Sallie* to Jefferson and Preston, Texas, consigning the goods to Steamboat Captain Gillet, for sale or barter. [2] The owner was at first skeptical of the outcome of these "ventures," as he called them, but apparently he was well-satisfied with the first trials. Late in May he sent ten more hogsheads on the *Little Sallie* to Red River. A few days later he consigned a large shipment of forty-nine hogsheads to the captain of the steamer *Louis D'or* on another run to the Red River. In return for the produce shipped on the *Louis D'or*, Palfrey received a number of hogs and a large quantity of "smoked middling." [3] By that time money had virtually disappeared, and the planter resorted willingly to barter. He continued throughout the summer and early fall to send his sugar north and west, trading it for various plantation necessities. This resourceful sugar producer was able to sell and trade his wares until his plantation fell in November of 1862 to Federal troops advancing up the Teche. His last transaction was on November 21 when he sold to Captain Boudreau of the steamer *Aichette* four hogsheads of sugar for $310 cash. At the time of this sale General Alfred Mouton's Confederate troops were in position on Palfrey's plantation, awaiting the arrival of the enemy at any moment. [4]

Most sugar growers explored every possibility in attempting to move their goods, and many of them were able to sell at least a small part of the 1861-1862 crop. Even after the Federal fleet was in possession of the lower Mississippi, a St. Mary Parish cane planter continued to ship his produce to Natchez by steamboat, where the sugar brought eight cents a pound and molasses twenty dollars a barrel. [5]

The experience of Governor Thomas O. Moore typified the complete

---

[1] John Moore to Reuben White, May 16, 1862, David Weeks and Family Papers.
[2] Palfrey Plantation Diary, May 12, 1862.
[3] *Ibid.*, May 27, June 6, 17, 1862.
[4] *Ibid.*, November 21, 1862.
[5] Minor Plantation Diary (1861-1865), August 7, 1862.

story of the sugar planters' unremitting search for markets. In June of 1862 the Governor sent twenty-five hogsheads of sugar to Jefferson, Texas, on the steamboat *Genl. Hodges* and seventeen hogsheads to Shreveport on the same vessel. Moore paid ten dollars a hogshead for transportation to Jefferson and eight dollars to Shreveport. The merchandise sold in Jefferson for $1,536, that in Shreveport for $950. These figures, reduced to value per pound, meant that sugar brought, after the cost of transportation was subtracted, a fraction over five cents a pound.[1] This was not a favorable profit, but by then New Orleans had fallen, and Moore could not sell his goods there at any figure. Two years later Moore, no longer governor, was a refugee from his Alexandria plantation, but he still had sugar to sell. In March an agent in Shreveport notified him that he could barter the produce for bacon if he wished to part with it in that way.[2] In the fall Moore attempted to salvage a remnant of his sugar by sending it into Texas. A permit issued by General E. Kirby Smith, commander of the Trans-Mississippi Department of the Confederacy, revealed the planter's plight: "Ex-Governor Thos O. Moore of Louisiana, has permission to take into Texas, and such point as he may select, sixty (60) hogsheads of sugar, which, together with the transportation required therefor, are exempted from impressment or interference."[3]

The prodigious efforts of the sugar cultivators to market their blockaded crop, though in many individual cases successful, were in general futile. Ingenuity and determination were not enough. The silent, relentless grip of the Federal navy shut off the vital arteries of the cane country. Unable to fall back on the railroads as a substitute for seaborne transportation, producers found the hasty improvisations of river shipping totally inadequate to the task of distributing the greatest yield in the history of the sugar industry. Even had they been able to ship their goods, the difficult problem of finding buyers among impoverished cotton planters still would have faced them. Invading Union soldiers found the sugar proprietors with their sugarhouses filled to overflowing and their pocketbooks and flour barrels empty as the bayou country fell into Northern control.

---

[1] Bill of lading of steamboat *Genl. Hodges* to Thomas O. Moore, June 24, 1862, Thomas O. Moore Papers.
[2] H. J. Phelps to Thomas O. Moore, March 29, 1864, Thomas O. Moore Papers.
[3] Special Order of General E. Kirby Smith, September 22, 1864, Thomas O. Moore Papers.

In April of 1862 the Federal army and navy struck at the exposed under area of the Confederacy in a combined land and water assault. Flag Officer David G. Farragut commanded the fleet, General Benjamin F. Butler the army. Two strongholds, Fort Jackson and Fort St. Philip, barred Farragut's approach on the Mississippi, but the rugged leader determined to run his ships past these fortifications. The folk of Magnolia Plantation a few miles up the river from the forts listened to the ominous bombardment that preceded Farragut's run and wondered what the future held in store for them. The overseer took the trouble to set down in his inimitable scrawl, "Herd a Tremendious Firing at Fort Jackson & St. Philup & presume the ... morter Fleet which is commanded by [Commander David D.] Porter Has Made the Long Look for an attack."[1] Farragut's drive up the river obviously came as no surprise to plantation inhabitants below the city.

As the Federal commander led his fleet under heavy fire past the thundering forts and up the river, inhabitants of the sugar plantations that lined the banks watched with mixed emotions. Effingham Lawrence, owner of Magnolia Plantation, had sent his family into New Orleans, presumably for safe-keeping. His vitriolic overseer had fled in fear before the Yankee advance. His Negroes crowded the levee in exquisite anticipation for a glimpse at the great pageant. The proud planter sat in his mansion and with a poise born of resignation wrote: "The Fleet are now passing the House... appear to be uninjured. They have burried a few Bodies in coming up a few miles below here—."[2] The most important conquest of Southern territory up to that time was under way.

To an invading soldier on the deck of one of the transports following in the wake of the fleet the scene was indelible. "We are no welcome tourists, at least not to the white inhabitants," he wrote. "Very few of them show themselves, and they do not answer our cheering, nor hardly look at us; they walk or ride grimly by, with faces set straight forward, as if they could thereby ignore our existence. But to the negroes we evidently appear as friends and redeemers. Such joyous gatherings of dark faces, such deep-chested shouts of welcome and deliverance, such a waving of green boughs and white vestments, and even of pickaninnies,

---

[1] *Magnolia Plantation Journal*, April 16, 1862.
[2] *Ibid.*, April 24, 1862.

such a bending of knees ... salutes our eyes ... as makes me grateful to Heaven for this hour of triumph." [1]

Most of the military manpower of Louisiana was in Tennessee and Virginia, fighting in the outer marches of the Confederacy to break the force of the Federal invasions by land. A small defending army under command of General Mansfield Lovell withdrew, and New Orleans lay exposed to Farragut's guns. Not bred in the tradition of fighting at the barricades, the authorities of the city, like those of other Southern communities later, surrendered to what appeared to them to be irresistible force. General Benjamin F. Butler disembarked his troops and began the most notorious military occupation of the Civil War. [2]

The presence of a Northern army in New Orleans put an end to Confederate control in the southernmost sugar parishes, leaving the planters of the area at the dubious mercy of General Butler. The mortification of these proud sugar proprietors is easily imagined. Some of them immediately fled from the invader. Determined not to live under a conqueror, they had decided even before New Orleans fell that they would go into exile in case of a successful Northern attack. This determination was brought about not only by pride, but also by economic expediency, for the planters were aware that their great investment in slaves would probably become worthless under military rule. General Butler's reputation for handling "contrabands"—a term which he earlier had applied to Negroes in conquered areas—preceded his arrival in the Crescent City.

When news of the fall of the city spread to surrounding parishes a flight from the plantations began. Perhaps one of the first to leave was J. B. Bond, described by the New Orleans *Daily Picayune* as one of the most energetic and successful sugar growers in Terrebonne Parish. This landowner fled to Texas early in the spring of 1862. [3] Inhabitants of the inland sugar regions, those not initially occupied by Northern troops, sometimes deserted homes before the invading armies reached them. One Bayou Lafourche family resolved to abandon the plantation if New Orleans should fall, and as it became increasingly clear that the city could not stand, elaborate preparations were made for flight. The proprietor chartered the steamboat *Lafourche*, loaded her with half of

---

[1] John W. De Forest, *Miss Ravenel's Conversion from Secession to Loyalty* (New York, 1939), 104. This novel was based on the author's experiences in the campaigns in lower Louisiana.

[2] James G. Randall, *The Civil War and Reconstruction* (New York, 1937), 580.

[3] New Orleans *Daily Picayune*, January 25, 1866.

the previous season's crop of sugar, and placed her in the bayou in front of the mansion. The crew maintained a full head of steam in the boilers, and the plantation folk were poised to leave on a moment's notice.

News of the surrender of New Orleans came the day after Farragut took possession of the city. Faithful to their resolution, the family boarded the *Lafourche* and made their way to Texas by way of Bayou Lafourche, the Mississippi River, and the Red River. A description by one of the members of this group left an unforgettable vision of the retreat of frightened and homeless sugar country citizens: "When we entered the Mississippi River it had become a seething mass of craft of all kinds and description that could be made into possible conveyances to carry away the terror-stricken people who were flying from their homes with their loved ones and treasures, all making a mad rush for the mouth of the Red River." [1] This account may have been exaggerated, but it conforms too closely to the unmistakable patterns of behavior in the wars of our own experience to be lightly discarded. Lower Louisiana presented the world with a preview of things to come—a glimpse at the heartbreaking spectacle of throngs of refugees seeking a distant and precarious sanctuary.

The example set by this family in departing from the region before a single blue uniform appeared on the bayou apparently was not followed by large numbers of their neighbors. Most Bayou Lafourche planters preferred to sit out the crisis, remaining on their land to await the unfolding of developments. The Federal army was engaged in consolidating its position in and around New Orleans during the summer of 1862 and did not immediately turn its attention to the outlying sugar parishes.

The complacency of the Bayou Lafourche plantation inhabitants was shortlived. By fall of 1862 General Butler was prepared to enlarge his sphere of operations and to grasp this rich section from the insecure hold of a small Confederate force stationed on the bayou. General Godfrey Weitzel was ordered to seize the region, and on October 24 moved down the stream from Donaldsonville. His invasion fell upon the Lafourche country like a lightning stroke from a black sky, driving General Alfred Mouton's Confederates from the area and placing the magnificent sugar plantations in the hands of the enemy. [2] Large numbers of landowners fled as the Northern formation closed in upon them, leaving

---

[1] Frances Fearn (ed.), *Diary of a Refugee* (New York, 1910), 15.

[2] *The War of the Rebellion; A Compilation of the Official Records of the Union and Confederate Armies*, 128 vols. (Washington, 1880-1901), Ser. I, Vol. XV, 158-180.

their homes and lands deserted and taking the best of their slaves with them to Texas.

If the planters had remained on their plantations and swallowed their pride, the great estates possibly would have fared far better than they did. Most Federal soldiers who commented on the war in the cane country were of this belief. One campaigner expressed this sentiment cogently in a novel dealing with operations in lower Louisiana: "Space fails us to tell of the sacking of this land of rich plantations; how the inhabitants, by flying before the northern Vandals, induced the spoliation of their own property; how the negroes defiled and plundered the forsaken houses, and how the soldiers thereby justified themselves in plundering the negroes; how the furniture, plate and libraries of the Lafourche planters were thus scattered upon the winds of destruction."[1] This same soldier put down a similar opinion in his reminiscences. He felt that if the proprietors had stayed in their houses they would have been provided military guards against the more flagrant vandalism. "The blacks," he recalled, "[had] the credit of doing most of the looting, and they in turn [were] looted by the *mauvais sujets* of the rank and file."[2] In many instances the property of men who remained at home did in fact escape with lighter damage than did places that were abandoned.

Regardless of how the plantations of the Lafourche region would have fared if owners had not fled, the fact was that many proprietors did leave in order to hold their slaves, and the deserted homes deteriorated at an alarming rate. Lack of care and the depredations of Negroes, foragers, and stragglers combined to strip them of their finery in short order. An observant Union officer set down an unexcelled description of the desolation visited upon the Lafourche country after the inhabitants fled: "I ride along the banked-up margin of Lafourche Bayou, by acres of abandoned plantations, through miles and leagues of cane fields."[3] This soldier examined a deserted plantation near the town of Houma, an estate said once to have possessed one of the finest libraries in Louisiana. The planter left the great book collection along with his broad fields, ripening crops, fine house, furniture, livestock, and many slaves, "all to the spoil of squatters, provost-marshals, soldiers, and camp-

---

[1] De Forest, *Miss Ravenel's Conversion from Secession to Loyalty*, 191.

[2] John W. De Forest, *A Volunteer's Adventures; a Union Captain's Record of the Civil War* (New Haven, 1946), 73.

[3] Alexander J. H. Duganne, *Camps and Prisons; Twenty Months in the Department of the Gulf* (New York, 1865), 49.

followers." The Northern campaigner was a booklover and he listened sorrowfully as Negroes told him of the destruction of the library, "how the books were scattered, mutilated, and consumed as fuel long ago." Rummaging through the silent rooms of the plantation mansion, he finally came upon a single volume in a littered chamber—"the last sad relic of that splendid library."[1]

Some of the more reflective Federal soldiers looked beyond the passions of the moment and grasped the import of the immense tragedy being enacted about them—the destruction of a graceful civilization. A contemplative Northern trooper apparently felt deep sorrow for planter exiles and considered with sadness the derelict plantations that lay in his path. Riding over the fields, he gathered vivid impressions to jot into his memoirs of conquest. His pen picture of a great estate captured perfectly the atmosphere of solitude and desertion that hung over the countryside: "The flowers are choking under grasp of rank weeks [and] rare fruit withers on unpruned limbs. The garden-walks are tangled, and a garden roller, in my path, is overrun with wild honeysuckles,... grass grows stirrup-high on the once beautiful lawn." And again: "Doors are swinging from jambs; roofs are falling in. Through a broken window of the sugar-house I see huge vats, half filled with molasses—thousands of gallons—soured and crusted with dust.... Out over the fields, with slackened bridle, I pursue the plantation-road, passing through miles of rotting cane, decadence of ungathered crops...."[2]

A writer who participated as a Northern officer in the Lafourche campaign recreated in virile prose a composite picture of an abandoned sugar plantation. The head of the family, wrote the author, had fallen leading a militia company at the battle of Georgia Landing, in which the Confederates had been expelled from the area. The family then gathered all of the Negroes they could find and "refugeed" to Texas. Then the field hands, who had hidden in the swamps to avoid being taken away, "... came upon the house like locusts of destruction, broke down its doors, shattered its windows, [and] plundered it from parlor to garret." They drank the contents of the wine cellar, and in drunken delight soiled the rich carpets, ripped up the furniture, and effaced the family portraits. "To the merely sentimental observer," reflected the writer, momentarily permitting his heart to overpower his mind, which

---

[1] *Ibid.*, 53.
[2] *Ibid.*, 34.

told him that the sins of slavery and rebellion deserved full avenging, "it was sad to think that this house of desolation had not long since been the abode of the generous family life and prodigal hospitality of a southern planter."[1]

The Mississippi River was the main cable through which the Federal military current flowed into the sugar land. Shortly after the seizure of New Orleans, Farragut paraded his fleet up the river. Plantations lining the banks of the stream were at the mercy of the stern invader's guns—a fact soon brought home violently to cane country folk. Farragut had made known his intention to fire upon plantation houses or towns that harbored bush-whackers. The fierce commander's vessels were shot at in August by partisan troopers in the vicinity of Donaldsonville, and true to his threat, Farragut swept the town with his "iron besoms of destruction."

This firm control of the Mississippi by the Union fleet, added to the fact that Baton Rouge was soon in enemy hands, caused many planters near the capital city to leave for unconquered parts of the Confederacy. The story of the abandonment of Arlington Plantation by the James McHatton family is an epic.

The McHattons made hasty but thorough preparations for the long and arduous journey to Texas. A rockaway carriage was altered so as to enable the family to sleep in it while camping along the trail. A cloth-covered wagon—similar to a prairie schooner—was loaded with provisions, and six of the plantation's best mules were stabled with harness hanging in readiness for instant flight. On the morning of December 17, 1862, the family saw Federal gunboats anchored in the river before Baton Rouge. A slave sent into the town to gather information returned with news that all who had harbored Confederates during the recent battle of Baton Rouge were to be arrested. James McHatton was guilty and knew that his seizure was but a matter of time. Throughout the day the mistress wandered through the rooms of the great house where she had spent so many happy years of her life. She bade farewell to a great collection of dinner and ball dresses, clothes that could not be taken on the journey into exile. Absent-mindedly she packed a trunk full of laces, flowers, and feathers—articles that were less than useless in her present extremity.

During the night of the seventeenth the Negro sugar maker from a

---

[1] De Forest, *Miss Ravenel's Conversion from Secession to Loyalty*, 223.

neighboring plantation brought word that the McHatton slaves were going over to the Northerners. Federal pickets on the adjoining place had told the Negroes that McHatton was to be arrested at daybreak. The husband instantly saddled his horse and rode through the woods to a rendezvous where his wife was to join him with the carriage and wagon the next morning. This decision proved to be a mistake.

The following morning the wife found the remaining blacks surly and disobedient, refusing to drive her to the appointed meeting place. One Negro man "had a misery in his back—had it ever since the crevasse." Another "never druv in his life-didn't [she] know he was de engineer?" Some of the Negroes said that one of the mules would not go, "that [Old Sal] was de balkinest mule on de place; she [would not] git a mile from [the house] 'fore she took de studs and wouldn't budge a step." At last one old servant named Dave agreed to drive the wagon until Old Sal balked. After hours of threatening, cajoling, and pleading, the mistress drove out of the yard. As she left, Aunt Hanna, an aged Negress who had been given a cabin in which to "sun away her half-blind ... old age," stood erect and proud in the door of her hut and cried, "Goodby madam—I b'ar you no malice."

The surging emotions of this vivacious plantation woman as she fled her beloved home before the whirlwind of the Northern invasion can be imagined, but no trace of bitterness stained her reminiscences as she stated: "So I rode away from Arlington, leaving the sugar-house crowded to its utmost capacity with the entire crop of sugar and molasses of the previous year for which we had been unable to find a market within 'our lines,' leaving cattle grazing in the fields, sheep wandering over the levee, doors and windows flung wide open, furniture in the rooms, clothes too fine for me to wear hanging in the armoires, china in the closets, pictures on the walls, beds unmade, table spread. It was late in the afternoon of that bright, clear day, December 18, 1862, that I bade Arlington adieu forever!"

For two days the determined woman eluded Federal patrols with her rockaway and improvised prairie schooner. She forced her reluctant Negro servant at pistol point to remain with her to drive the wagon. On the third day she struck a broad highway filled with wagons loaded with "furniture, beds, bundles, cooking-utensils ... and barrels overflowing with hastily collected household effects...." Bedraggled mothers with troops of cold and miserable children tramped the dusty road. Thus the "rearguard ... of an army of wretched citizens fleeing from their broken homes" laboriously wended its way toward Texas and exile.[1]

The Mississippi River Coast from New Orleans to Baton Rouge wore the stern aspect of abandonment and ruin. Shaken by this evidence of the wages of war, a Northern army chaplain in 1863 wrote: "If you leave the city, and take the level road to Baton Rouge ... the desolation becomes all the more marked. There is not a single planter in the department who has not personally suffered through this war. Their crops of sugar-cane, yielding from five hundred to a thousand hogsheads of sugar, are still standing in February; and there is no hope of saving them, for the frost has been at work on them. Cane is standing now in March; thousands and tens of thousands of acres of it. Thus the crop of the past year is nothing; and that of the coming year will be the same."[2]

Farther north along the Mississippi the story of desertion and waste was reminiscent of that in the lower reaches of the sugar country. A Federal soldier stationed near Port Hudson in the summer of 1863 was depressed at the neglect that he saw in the fine sugar plantations there. After describing the deterioration of one of these estates he continued in a letter to his family: "The amount the people have lost must be incalculable. Northern people do not understand how thankful they ought to be that their section of the country is not the seat of war. One must see the ruin to judge of it." This sympathetic invader, whose words have such a disturbingly current ring, was moved at sight of the elegant mansions abandoned by owners and pillaged by Negroes and men of both armies.[3]

Planters in the northern rim of the cane land escaped the rigors of invasion until 1863, but in the spring of that year General Nathaniel P. Banks carried the war along Bayou Teche and into the Red River Valley, capturing Alexandria in Rapides Parish. Sugar growers whose land lay in the path of the Federal advance followed the example of flight set months earlier by their brethren of the lower Mississippi and Lafourche sections. Great numbers of Bayou Teche proprietors pushed westward into Texas with their slaves.[4] Colonel A. J. Fremantle, an English military observer passing through Confederate Louisiana in May, was witness to the coffles of Negroes being hurried out of the

---

[1] Ripley, *From Flag to Flag*, 51-63, *passim*.
[2] George Hughes Hepworth, *The Whip, Hoe, and Sword; or, the Gulf Department in '63* (Boston, 1864), 92.
[3] William Fowler, *Memorials of William Fowler* (New York, 1875), 60.
[4] Sitterson, *Sugar Country*, 215.

state. On the morning of the tenth he observed: "The road today was alive with negroes, who were being 'run' into Texas out of Banks' way. We must have met hundreds of them, and many families of planters, who were much to be pitied, especially the ladies." [1]

By the end of 1862 neglect and abandonment were rampant in the cane country. The New Orleans *Daily Picayune* took sympathetic notice of the plight of citizens of this section, trenchantly defining the awful choice facing planters throughout the war. The editor declared in gloomy periods: "The poor people of the interior—and by this phrase we mean all who are found upon the confines of disputed authority in Louisiana—are in most trying straits. They are between two fires; and, in many instances, can hardly escape either partial or complete destruction but by fleeing from their homes, and leaving them scenes of desolation—mournful mementoes of what the war has brought upon the people. The crops are left unharvested. The servants are demoralized and reduced to starvation and sickness. Property of all kinds goes to ruin. The members of the family seek a precarious living among distant friends." [2]

For the sugar planters, the gay, light days of faraway war were ended. No longer did they relax on their verandas, drinking mint juleps and discoursing on the ineffectiveness of naval blockade and the impending collapse of the Northern economy. Gone were the dangerous illusions concerning the pre-eminence of King Cotton and the invincibility of Southern arms. The Mississippi—friend and benefactor in time of peace—had betrayed them in time of war and had borne the invader into their midst. Mansions stood empty and pillaged, with idle sugarhouses falling rapidly into ruin. Cane fields were littered with rottenness. Desolation brooded over the plantation country.

---

[1] A. J. Fremantle, *Three Months in the Southern States; April-June, 1863* (New York, 1864), 45.

[2] New Orleans *Daily Picayune*, December 4, 1862.

CHAPTER VI

WINDS OF DESTRUCTION

For three weary years during the war lower Louisiana was fixed in the stern pillory of military occupation, and the plantation country was filled with violence. The southern parishes, and those farther north that lay along the Mississippi River, were within the sphere of effective Federal control, while the western and northern stretches of the cane land—parishes along Bayou Teche and the Red River—were disputed territory. Possession of this interior zone swayed to and fro between the contending armies. On two occasions the Union army thrust into the Red River Valley, only to recoil on its bases along the Mississippi. It will be recalled that in the spring of 1863 General Banks sent a raiding column as far north as Alexandria in Rapides Parish. One year later this Union leader made his ill-fated Red River campaign—a determined effort to conquer the central and western marches of the state. Defeated by Confederate General Richard Taylor in the battles of Mansfield and Pleasant Hill, he withdrew to the south.[1]

The Bayou Teche country played a unique part in military operations in Louisiana. Whereas the Mississippi was the line along which rolled the great right wheel of the invasion of the sugar land, the Teche bore the Federals along the region's left flank. A Northern participant in the conquest caught a striking similarity between the role of the Teche land in the war in Louisiana and that of the Shenandoah Valley in the conflict in Virginia. To this soldier-observer, "The Teche country was a sort of a back alley, parallel to the main street wherein the heavy fighting must go on; and one side or the other was always running up and down the Teche with the other in full chase after it."[2]

Federal supremacy in the Bayou Lafourche territory was fixed as the result of General Weitzel's campaign in the fall of 1862. Temporarily in the summer of 1863, however, the Confederates recaptured this rich sugar region. At that time General U. S. Grant was closing the vise on Vicksburg, and General Banks was besieging Port Hudson, the secondary

---

[1] Richard Taylor, *Destruction and Reconstruction; Personal Experiences of the Late War* (New York, 1879), 162-171, *passim*.
[2] De Forest, *A Volunteer's Adventures*, 85.

Confederate stronghold on the lower Mississippi. Confederate leaders matured a bold plan to relieve the beleaguered fortresses. General Richard Taylor was to launch a counterattack in lower Louisiana, striking at the city of New Orleans, with the strategic objective of forcing Banks away from Port Hudson in order that the Confederate army there might escape and join General Joseph E. Johnston at Jackson, Mississippi, for an assault on Grant.

In June Taylor's forces burst into the Lafourche area like an avenging flame. One wing advanced to the bayou below Donaldsonville and thrust south along the stream, while another captured Brashear City [1] on the lower Atchafalaya. These two segments of Taylor's army then converged upon a Union garrison at Bayou Boeuf, forcing it to surrender. This series of movements placed most of the Bayou Lafourche plantation region in Taylor's hands, and permitted the "shaggy ponies and long, lank, dirty mosstroopers" of the Confederate cavalry to scour the countryside. Taylor threatened New Orleans. Would the feint lure Banks from Port Hudson?

The audacious maneuver was of no avail. Banks refused to strike at the bait; Vicksburg and Port Hudson surrendered. Banks then quickly concentrated at Donaldsonville at the head of Bayou Lafourche and prepared to fall upon the Confederate forces. Taylor did not await this eventuality, but discreetly slipped away to the northwestern reaches of the state. [2]

While sugar growers and their sons rode to war throughout the entire Confederacy, the plantations themselves sometimes were the stage for battles in the sugar land. Cane fields became battlefields as the armies contended for supremacy along the lower Mississippi, bringing the war home to the civilian population—even to plantation wives and children. The skirmish of Georgia Landing in the fall of 1862 occurred on a Bayou Lafourche sugar estate. [3]

William T. Palfrey of St. Mary Parish witnessed the conversion of his own property into a battleground. His diary tells the story of the combined land and water assault of the Federals along the Teche early in 1863. In November of the previous year Federal gunboats began to probe up this stream and to fire upon the Confederate steamer *Cotton*, which was located on the bayou by Palfrey's land. Throughout the

---

[1] Now Morgan City, Louisiana.
[2] *The War of the Rebellion*, Ser. I, Vol. XXVI, Pt. I, 46-52, 186-232.
[3] *Ibid.*, Vol. XV, 158-180.

remainder of 1862 desultory firing continued between the *Cotton* and her adversaries. Palfrey developed great admiration for the officers and men of the Confederate steamer and once wrote, "Our only defences seem to be Capt. Fuller of the *Cotton*, a gallant officer, & his crew." On January 1, 1863, the planter recorded that upon one occasion when the Federal fleet engaged the *Cotton*, the invaders were driven off by the Pelican Battery of flying artillery; he was elated to see the enemy move back to Berwick Bay "in double quick time."

The *Cotton* met her end only a few days later, and Palfrey sorrowfully penned an account of her defeat: "About 8 A.M. a heavy bombardment took place between the enemy's gun Boats on the one side, & the gun Boat 'Cotton' on the other—which lasted about 2 hours, in which Capt. Fuller of the latter was wounded in both arms, & [a lieutenant] killed. 4 or 6 of the men were Killed & 12 or 13 wounded—The enemy's gun Boats were Kept back by the obstructions at ... the bridge—... During the night, the heavy guns were taken from the 'Cotton'—She was sent down to below the fortifications & there sank for an obstruction & upper work burned, by order from our general."

In April of 1863 a skirmish occurred on Palfrey's plantation between the Federal column pushing north to Alexandria and General Alfred Mouton's brigade, which disputed the Northern advance. On January 13 couriers brought information of Federal troop landings in force at Berwick Bay. This intelligence sent the Confederates, who were encamped on Palfrey's land, into entrenchments on his "lower line." Two days later fighting raged on the plantation of P. C. Bethell below Palfrey's place, during which the Bethell mansion was burned to the ground by the Confederates, and Mouton drove his foe back to Berwick Bay. Throughout February the Southern troops remained in camp on Palfrey's premises. From time to time battle appeared imminent. By the tenth the planter was sufficiently disturbed to sell $5,000 worth of copper pans, worms, tanks, and pipes from his sugarhouse. The buyer, a man from St. Martinville, was to take delivery as the equipment stood and to provide for disassembling and removing it, all at his "peril & risk."

On April 12 began the fight which so long had threatened. With Thucydidean detachment, Palfrey chronicled events at the scene of battle: "April 12, 1863, At 3 P.M. The engagement commenced—& lasted with vigor about an hour & an half—Our troops were principally within our entrenchments—The enemy were repulsed & driven back—with what loss I do not know—Our loss trifling, if any.—The great struggle is reported to come tomorrow—April 13, The engagement was renewed this morning at 7 O'clock & has lasted all day—The firing on both sides very heavy—Our troops have stood their ground, tho assailed by 4 times their number.—April 14, A flank movement on the part of the enemy (who have landed in large forces at [a neighboring plantation] has forced our troops to retreat.—They are marching every thing up the Bayou).... Our troops followed by the enemy passed through [Franklin?] at different periods today till 2 P.M.—."[1]

Fighting in fields of sugar cane was an experience never to be forgotten by those who participated in it. The charge of General Weitzel's brigade against the Confederate position on the Teche passed through a vast expanse of the tall cane, which formed an "inextricable chevaux de frise" against the advance. The organization moved toward the Confederate works in a long, single line that stretched from a wooded area on the left to the water's edge on the right. Nature seemed to fight against the invaders as they pushed forward, "prostrating or climbing fences, and struggling amid horrible labyrinths of tangled sugar cane."[2]

Other Union campaigners met with the formidable obstacle of miles of thick cane during the action along Bayou Lafourche in the summer of 1863. On July 20 a Federal brigade moving south from Donaldsonville was surprised by the Confederates and driven in haste back to the town. A Northern soldier who tasted this little defeat had his first view of the Southerners when he observed squads of them moving through rows of cane on three sides of him. The Federals took advantage of the one free side to retreat toward Donaldsonville. In the words of a panic-stricken lad: "Confusion became worse confounded. Every attempt to keep in line failed, and in squads or alone, we pressed to the rear. It was a day of utter exhaustion. Pressing through corn ten feet high, the sun pouring down on us, unable to catch a mouthful of air, was bad enough, but we found scratching our way through the cane-fields tenfold worse. Cane [presents] an almost impenetrable jungle. Four miles, measured by rods, forty, as computed by discomfort and fatigue, passed over and we reached the river, some near the fort, at Donaldsonville...."[3]

Plantation women often witnessed the violence of war on or near

---

[1] Palfrey Plantation Diary, November 16, December 31, 1862, January 13-15, February 10, April 12-14, 1863.

[2] De Forest, *A Volunteer's Adventures*, 87.

[3] Henry T. Johns, *Life with the Forty-ninth Massachusetts Volunteers* (Pittsfield, Massachusetts, 1864), 337.

the sugar domains. During the night of March 14, 1863, Confederate troops defending Port Hudson, Louisiana, fought off a Union sally. "Such an incessant roar," exclaimed an excited girl at nearby Linwood Plantation as the clamor of the skirmish mounted in intensity. At every cannon discharge the plantation house shook on its foundation. Women clustered about a window from which they watched the "incessant flash of guns and the great shooting stars of flame, which [were] the hot shot of the enemy." They thrilled at sight of burning houses in the distance.[1]

Union naval control of Louisiana's waterways placed sugar plantations under the muzzles of enemy guns, and from time to time the Federals pressed this advantage by shelling establishments, sometimes for harboring snipers, again perhaps out of sheer deviltry. Gunboats dropped shells into the lawn of nearby Arlington Plantation throughout the night following the battle of Baton Rouge.[2] During this same engagement the steamer *Essex* fired upon the plantations near the capital city.[3] At one time during the war a Federal officer lobbed cannon balls at The Cottage, the plantation house of his cousin near Baton Rouge.[4] In November of 1862 a Louisiana girl charged as she listened to gunfire on the Mississippi, "The [Northerners] are banging away on some treasonable sugar-houses that are disobedient enough to grind cane on the other side of the river."[5]

Sugar plantations frequently served as camps for both armies. William T. Palfrey's plantation on the Teche was for months the camp site of General Alfred Mouton's brigade of the Confederate army. The General made the Palfrey mansion his headquarters, and when General Richard Taylor, commander of all Confederate forces in Louisiana, visited camp he enjoyed the hospitality of this house. During the campaign up the Teche in 1863 General Nathaniel P. Banks of the Union army made his headquarters at The Shadows, the plantation mansion of the David Weeks family. David Weeks' widow died in this great house while it was occupied by the Federal commander.[6]

Federal outposts and garrisons often were established on abandoned sugar domains. In August of 1864 a skirmish of unusual interest occurred

---

[1] Sarah Morgan Dawson, *A Confederate Girl's Diary* (New York, 1913), 337.
[2] Ripley, *From Flag to Flag*, 41.
[3] Dawson, *A Confederate Girl's Diary*, 161.
[4] Work Projects Administration, *Louisiana; a Guide to the State*, 524.
[5] Dawson, *A Confederate Girl's Diary*, 289.
[6] Work Projects Administration, *Louisiana; a Guide to the State*, 314.

on a sugar plantation near Donaldsonville. A Major Remington commanded the Union detachment on outpost duty at this estate. One dark night a Confederate force crept upon the unsuspecting Northerners, and the Confederate leader sent Remington a demand for unconditional surrender. The Union officer rejected this overture and succeeded in cutting his way through to Donaldsonville. In the Southern unit was the son of the owner of the plantation, a young man who bitterly hated Remington and had once sent him a challenge to duel. The offer had been ignored by the Federal officer allegedly because "... he was too wise to give his enemy his wish and risk a valuable life in a senseless encounter." The rash plantation youth had sworn to avenge the seizure of his father's property by killing the Federal officer on sight, and the threat was almost consummated on the night of the engagement. Seeing an officer whom he took to be Remington, the Southerner fired. He hit his mark, but the unfortunate victim was the wrong man, and the major escaped unscathed. [1]

Both armies requisitioned plantation mansions or sugarhouses as hospitals during battle. In January of 1863 William T. Palfrey took into his home an eighteen-year-old boy who was sick, providing the lad with a pleasant room and tenderly caring for him. Not long before this time Palfrey had received news of the death of his own son in combat, a blow that possibly made him more sensitive to the suffering of soldiers in the field. [2] Immediately before the encounter on the Palfrey plantation in April the medical staff of General Mouton's brigade requested both mansion and sugarhouse for use as hospitals. Palfrey willingly assented. [3]

The Federal army investing Port Hudson in the summer of 1863 converted nearby plantation buildings and grounds into field hospitals. [4] A member of the invading force left this classic of brutal realism in describing one of these improvised hospitals: "In the centre of this mass of suffering stood several operating tables, each burdened by a grievously wounded man and surrounded by surgeons and their assistants. Underneath were great pools of clotted blood, amidst which lay amputated fingers, hands, arms, feet and legs, only a little more ghastly in color

---

[1] Henry Murray Calvert, *Reminiscences of a Boy in Blue, 1862-1865* (New York, 1920), 203-207.
[2] Palfrey Plantation Diary, January 2, 1863.
[3] *Ibid.*, April 12, 1863.
[4] Caroline Lloyd (ed.), *A Memorial of Lieutenant Daniel Perkins Dewey, of the Twenty-fifth Regiment, Connecticut Volunteers* (Hartford, 1864), 103.

than the faces of those who waited their turn on the table. The surgeons, who never ceased their awful labor, were daubed with blood to the elbows; and a smell of blood drenched the stifling air, overpowering even the pungent odor of chloroform. The place resounded with groans, notwithstanding that most of the injured men who retained their senses exhibited the heroic endurance so common on the battle-field. One man, whose leg was amputated close to his body, uttered an inarticulate jabber of broken screams, and rolled, or rather bounced from side to side of a pile of loose cotton, with such violence that two hospital attendants were fully occupied in holding him. Another, shot through the body, lay speechless and dying, but quivering from head to foot with a prolonged though probably unconscious agony. He continued to shudder thus for half an hour, when he gave one super-human throe, and then lay quiet forever." [1]

Sugar estates frequently became refugee camps to civilians driven from their hearths by the fury of war, while destitute families of soldiers went from plantation to plantation begging food. [2] Southern travelers shunned towns along the river, because these were points of Federal control, seeking hospitality at the plantations. The frequency of these demands upon a plantation mistress near Baton Rouge was so great that finally she set aside two rooms in the rear of the house for the convenience of these weary journeyers. [3] Inhabitants of cities sometimes were for months guests of planter friends after the coming of the invading army. The women of a prominent Baton Rouge family fled first to the Nolan plantation a few miles from the capital city, but they soon departed to the tune of a hostile cannonade and took haven at Linwood Plantation within Confederate territory near Port Hudson. [4]

A most interesting case of a sugar estate serving as a resort for homeless victims of war was that of Arlington Plantation before it was abandoned. During the battle of Baton Rouge in the summer of 1862 the mistress stood at her bedroom window watching the bombardment of the capital city. Suddenly, what appeared to be a herd of stampeded sheep came before her eyes. A moment later she discerned that these were not sheep, but human beings, "swelling and surging, and rushing in the wildest hurry and flight, through a volume of dust made ten times

---

[1] De Forest, *Miss Ravenel's Conversion from Secession to Loyalty*, 257-258.
[2] Shugg, *Origins of Class Struggle in Louisiana*, 183-184.
[3] Ripley, *From Flag to Flag*, 44.
[4] Dawson, *A Confederate Girl's Diary*, 145-147.

more stifling by the fierce heat." These were a host of civilian refugees driven from their homes in the embattled city. Panting and pushing, they hurled themselves upon Arlington Plantation for sanctuary. "They poured into our gates and invaded the house," recalled the mistress. "A small army...of terrified human beings—all roused from their beds by firing and fighting in the very streets; rushing half-clad from houses being riddled with shot and shell."

The hostess struggled valiantly to feed "a great multitude with five loaves and no fishes." The men foraged, bringing in sheep and oxen which they butchered and cooked on the plantation lawn. Bits of smoked meat were passed among the famished people, and babies were given pieces of meat to suck. Twelve pounds of tea in the pantry soon disappeared. The men brought immense iron kettles, customarily used for making soap, to the lawn, converting them into improvised teapots. Fires roared under the kettles, and the refugees drank tea "ad libitum." The plantation mistress' heart went out to expectant mothers caught simultaneously in the travail of war and of childbirth. She recalled, "Time and time again Charlotte [a slave woman], who was the Lady Bountiful of the occasion, came to tell me that first one, then another, and still another poor woman was in peril and little garments went from my scanty store to the innocent babes who opened their eyes on that eventful day, and nothing but the supreme terror of their mothers prevented them from first seeing light amid scenes of carnage and desolation." [1]

A deserted sugar plantation served in the perhaps unique capacity of an improvised parole camp. In October of 1863 paroled Confederate soldiers set up Camp Crow on a cane plantation two miles from Alexandria. The troops selected the most commodious of the Negro cabins and converted them into barracks. Benches and bunks were constructed to add to the convenience of the place. Cavalry mounts and artillery horses occupied plantation stables. A short distance from the makeshift barracks was a field of ripening sugar cane, untouched by the departed owner. One of the daily tasks of the soldiers was to fill a cart with cane and distribute it among the members of the camp. A resident of Camp Crow recalled that a favorite method of passing the long days was chewing sugar cane. [2]

---

[1] Ripley, *From Flag to Flag*, 34-38.

[2] William H. Tunnard, *A Southern Record; the History of the Third Regiment Louisiana Infantry* (Baton Rouge, 1866), 310.

To many Northern soldiers, sugar plantations with their mansions and elaborate sugarhouses were rich plunder. Men who had a destructive urge in their make-up found ample objects in the cane country upon which to release their energy. Some members of the invading army were fired with a zeal to destroy Southern property, feeling that this devastation was just retribution to planters for the sins of slavery and rebellion. This sentiment often appeared in letters written home by soldiers "engaged in the noble crusade to stamp out human bondage." One humanitarian invader stated that he and his comrades were shivering under thin blankets in Louisiana, "waiting for orders to strike a blow that [would] prostrate that whole institution, which [built] for a few oppressors such mansions, while it [doomed] the entire peasantry of the land, black and white, to hopeless poverty and wretchedness." [1]

The Northern army brought no policy of Assyrian frightfulness into the bayou land; it did not visit upon defeated inhabitants a wholesale, premeditated destruction of homes and other plantation property. Invading troops did, nevertheless, from time to time wantonly burn and otherwise despoil houses in scattered areas of the cane country. In the spring of 1862, for example, a detachment of the Twenty-first Indiana Infantry fired the dwelling house and sugarhouse of Planter J. B. Bond of Terrebonne Parish, "leaving the plantation a smoking ruin." [2] A St. Mary Parish planter charged the Union army with burning houses in 1863 as it retreated from a skirmish on the Teche. [3] Troops sent from Mississippi to reinforce General Banks in 1864 burned houses said to be flying Confederate flags near the mouth of the Red River. [4]

The Red River area perhaps suffered more actual destruction than any other part of the sugar land. The beaten army that General Banks brought back from the battles of Mansfield and Pleasant Hill in 1864 burned sugarhouses, gins, and factories in its path. [5] Governor Henry W. Allen saw the track of the withdrawing enemy as one scene of desolation, charging that while Alexandria was in flames, Federal General Andrew J. Smith rode among his men exulting, "Boys, this looks like

---

[1] Johns, *Life with the Forty-ninth Massachusetts Volunteers*, 164.
[2] New Orleans *Daily Picayune*, January 25, 1866.
[3] Palfrey Plantation Diary, January 15, 1863.
[4] E. Newsome, *Experience in the War of the Great Rebellion* (Carbondale, Illinois, 1879), 65.
[5] G. P. Whittington, "Rapides Parish, Louisiana; a History," *Louisiana Historical Quarterly*, XVIII (January, 1935), 38.

war!"[1] A prominent citizen of Rapides Parish who was an eyewitness to the treatment meted out to his section gave insight into the behavior of the hostile army: "It cannot therefore excite surprise in the minds of any, that the line of march of the army under General Banks can be traced like an Indian war trail, or the fire path of the prairie—by smouldering ruins of villages, dwellings, gins, and sugar-houses—the conversion of a rich, beautiful and highly improved agricultural region into a vast wilderness."[2] This fiery accusation doubtless was exaggerated, the word "wilderness" an overstatement. It conforms too closely, however, with the testimony of other onlookers to be ignored.

A greater loss occurred in the sugar country from what might be called petty vandalism than from the burning of property. Observers on the spot never failed to point up this form of destruction. A Vermont campaigner described the stripping of General Richard Taylor's estate. "I wish you could have seen the soldiers plunder this plantation," the writer declared. "The camp-kettle and pans I intend to send home, ... they are made of heavy tin, covered with copper." This soldier ended with a word about devastation in the entire Lafourche area: "All kinds of the best mahogany furniture [are] broken to pieces. Nothing is respected."[3] A Connecticut volunteer drew a perfect picture of the treatment often given these estates by Federal pickets. He was stationed on a plantation near Baton Rouge, "where not an article of furniture, not a door & scarcely a window remain[ed] in the house." The sentries had decorated the wall with "hieroglyphics & autographs," and Negro cabins and fences had been consumed as fuel.[4] A Northern officer, possibly smitten by conscience, lamented that the once prosperous region about Thibodaux was being laid waste; that Negroes and soldiers roamed everywhere, breaking into and plundering plantation houses, and "destroying furniture, books and pictures in mere wantonness."[5]

The burning of fence rails for fuel was a severe blow to planters in a day before the invention of wire fences. Most sugar establishments were enclosed by fences of cypress rails which made excellent fires, and thousands of Yankee soldiers burned them in order to warm themselves

---

[1] Sarah Anne Dorsey, *Recollections of Henry Watkins Allen; Brigadier-General Confederate States Army, Ex-Governor of Louisiana* (New York, 1866), 279.

[2] Whittington, "Rapides Parish, Louisiana; a History," *Louisiana Historical Quarterly*, XVIII (January, 1935), 38.

[3] *De Bow's Review*, II, N. S. (November, 1866), 538.

[4] New Orleans *Daily True Delta*, March 8, 1863.

[5] De Forest, *A Volunteer's Adventures*, 73-74.

and heat their rations. Personal reminiscences and contemporary military accounts abounded in stories woven around the procuring of these rails. Every time a certain Federal division halted during the Teche campaign of 1863, each man seized a piece of the nearest fence, and within a few minutes innumerable fires were heating coffee and broiling slices of salt pork.[1] An accomplished Yankee storyteller declared that his division had a streak of aestheticism in it—a fastidiousness that made the men abhor the fact that the zig-zag fences were out of line. When the formation halted, members grabbed the nearest fence in order to straighten it. Planter-owners complained to headquarters, whereupon an order descended that only the top rail of a fence should be taken. "The Nineteenth Corps adopted the order," asserted this soldier, "and took only the top rail as each one found them and the result was we got there just the same."[2]

Impressment of horses and mules by the invaders was an irreparable blow which no planter escaped. When the Federals visited Duncan Kenner's Ashland Plantation in the summer of 1862 they took away all of his race horses and mules. William J. Minor's blooded horses were seized at the same time.[3] The New Orleans *Daily True Delta* asserted that in July of 1863 an expedition to the western sugar parishes netted the Northerners 3,000 mules and horses,[4] and Union soldiers on the Teche in November of 1863 reported that great herds of horses and mules were being driven from the plantations.[5]

An observer who traveled up the Mississippi as far as Baton Rouge in 1863 neatly summarized the problem regarding the seizing of livestock: "The planters' horses have all been stolen, their mules and teams have all been confiscated. They stand in the midst of their great plantations, with the interest on a heavy mortgage staring them in the face, perfectly powerless ... Uncle Sam with more than his usual foresight and severity, has pressed into the service of his soldiers the whole mule-force of the department."[6]

Federal troops stripped Louisiana plantations of an untold amount of

---

[1] Charles B. Johnson, *Muskets and Medicine; or Army Life in the Sixties* (Philadelphia, 1917), 147.
[2] Frank M. Flinn, *Campaigning with Banks in Louisiana* (Lynn, Massachusetts, 1887), 20.
[3] Minor Plantation Diary (1861-1862), August 23, 1863.
[4] New Orleans *Daily True Delta*, July 3, 1863.
[5] Lawrence Van Alstyne, *Diary of an Enlisted Man* (New Haven, 1910), 226.
[6] Hepworth, *Whip, Hoe, and Sword*, 92.

property by foraging and looting. In April of 1863, for example, over 100 army teams stopped for the night at one of William J. Minor's places, consuming and carrying away 250 barrels of corn and a large quantity of hay.[1] Northerners stationed at Donaldsonville in 1863 feasted on chickens, tomatoes, figs, milk, and fresh meat. "On July 12," one Federal stated, "[soldiers] went up the river about two miles on a foraging expedition ... [and] cleaned things out good." A trooper at Baton Rouge referred to foraging along Highland Road, where in a ten-mile stretch he and his comrades took sixty barrels of molasses and five hogsheads of sugar.[2] In the vicinity of Port Hudson, pillaging expeditions scoured the countryside, frequently remaining out for days at a time. These men "had to steel their hearts against the entreaties and protests of the rebel women," whose plantations they robbed.[3]

Federal units on the Teche in 1863 lived off the land. "Enormous sweet potatoes could be had for the digging; oranges grew along the road plentifully as apples in Ohio," remembered one campaigner, and poultry was so abundant that army rations were discarded.[4] Northern soldiers on Bayou Vermilion in 1863 foraged "like the locusts of Revelation."[5]

Food-gathering expeditions could be hazardous. In October of 1863 a party of Northerners was surprised and captured on a Bayou Teche sugar plantation. The patrol members were absorbed in eating dinner and relaxed their security measures. Confederate cavalrymen crept upon them, capturing their muskets, which were stacked unguarded in the yard, and making prisoners of the entire lot.[6]

The looting of sugarhouses often became an occasion of frolic and festivity. In January of 1863 a Union organization unburdening plantations near Plaquemine of their sugar and molasses turned the affair into a molasses-candy expedition. "Over every camp-fire," reminisced a participant, "was a kettle of molasses, and along in the morning the boys

---

[1] Minor Plantation Diary (1863), August 12.
[2] Rodney W. Torrey, *War Diary of Rodney W. Torrey, 1862-1863* (n.p., n.d.), 44, 63.
[3] J. S. Clark, *Life in the Middle West* (Chicago, 1916), 100.
[4] Albert O. Marshall, *Army Life; from a Soldier's Journal* (Joliet, 1884), 291. For other interesting accounts of foraging along the Teche, see William H. Bentley, *History of the Seventy-seventh Illinois Volunteer Infantry* (Peoria, 1883), 207; and Frank H. Mason, *The Forty-second Ohio Infantry; a History of the Organization and Services of that Regiment in the War of the Rebellion* (Cleveland, 1876), 243.
[5] De Forest, *A Volunteer's Adventures*, 156.
[6] Mason, *The Forty-second Ohio Infantry*, 243-244.

were busily engaged ... pulling candy."[1] When General Banks pushed to Alexandria in 1863 his soldiers foraged widely for provisions. Cattle, hogs, and sheep in great numbers were taken by hungry troops.[2] During the 1864 campaign up the Red River, General Banks ordered that sugarhouses should not be molested and placed guards to enforce the measure, but enterprising Yankee soldiers were not to be denied, and these sentries were "flanked" by thousands of men. When the troops moved out the next morning large quantities of sugar were left on the ground.[3]

Plantation furniture and fixtures were handsome booty to Northern men and officers alike. In September of 1862 all of the silver was stolen from Bradish Johnson's plantation on the Mississippi below New Orleans.[4] The Opelousas *Courier* charged on September 20 that "a robbing expedition" had cleaned many places along the Mississippi of all moveable property.[5] The memoirs of a soldier-looter provide a classic account of a "strike" made on a rich sugar estate: "We rushed in like a flock of sheep, and secured everything of value. The Captain and I got two nice chairs, a table, a wash-basin, a stone-jug, tin measures, and a half-barrel of molasses.... We gave a gracious permission to some poor whites nearby, who had kept aloof from the sugar-house out of fear of the owner, to help themselves ad libitum. Their eyes bunged out with joy, and in they went. We confiscated a donkey and cart and proceeded to load up. Several others afterwards reached the spot and grabbed right and left.... The returning troop was headed by the donkey and cart, laden with old furniture of every kind.... As the donkey was unaccommodating, an officer walked at his side to help the driver effect a forward movement. Behind, a half-dozen captains and lieutenants marched, shouldering chairs, sweet potatoes, pots, pans, kettles, and other articles of domestic utility, and in this form we passed the guard and entered camp, and laid down our plunder in readiness for tent-pitching."[6]

---

[1] Flinn, *Campaigning with Banks in Louisiana*, 15.

[2] G. P. Whittington (ed.), "Concerning the Loyalty of Slaves in Louisiana in 1863," *Louisiana Historical Quarterly*, XIV (October, 1931), 489.

[3] John M. Gould, *History of the First- Tenth- Twenty-ninth Maine Regiment* (Portland, 1871), 406.

[4] Sitterson, "Magnolia Plantation, 1852-1862; a Decade of a Louisiana Sugar Estate," *Mississippi Valley Historical Review*, XXV (September, 1938), 208-209.

[5] Opelousas *Courier*, September 20, 1862.

[6] Fowler, *Memorials of William Fowler*, 21-22.

According to local folklore, the pillaging of Duncan Kenner's lavish Ashland Plantation in Ascension Parish provided an incident of unusual interest. Kenner had hidden a vast quantity of wines and liquors under the floor of his plantation pigeon-house. After the spoilers had cleaned the wine cellar of what little resources were left in it by the owner, they reconnoitered for additional spirits. The cache in the pigeon-house finally was discovered. Tradition has it that drunken soldiers scattered along all of the roads in the vicinity of the plantation, and that the jails of Ascension Parish were filled to overflowing with imbibers. A large stock of intoxicants was shipped by steamboat to nearby officers' quarters, where the Northerners had a "halcyon and vociferous time." [1]

Suger planters endured seizures by friend as well as foe. On many occasions Confederates sacked and pillaged in a manner that would have reflected credit on the Yankees. [2] William J. Minor in 1862 complained that a Confederate general refused to pay for provisions taken from Terrebonne Parish establishments for use of the Confederacy. [3] A Rapides Parish resident wrote to Governor Thomas O. Moore in May of 1863 that the crop would be lost if Confederate military authorities refused to release mules that they had seized. The Southerners also took meat and other supplies from the plantations. [4] Federal soldiers stationed at Port Hudson in the summer of 1863 found that sugar plantations near this battered town had been stripped by Southern as well as Northern armies. [5] William J. Minor mourned in the fall of 1864 that "the Rebs" had taken the remainder of his thoroughbred horses. [6]

The most damning evidence of Confederate looting came from the accusing pen of William T. Palfrey. This Bayou Teche planter suffered for months the pilfering and stealing of a Southern organization encamped upon his land. As an eyewitness to these misdemeanors, he recorded, "The brigade ... returned to their camping ground on my place & resumed their usual habits of depredation." Over a month later he stated, "The brigade of Genl. Alfred (Mouton) is still encamped on my plantation, devastating my property; robbing & plundering me & my negro cabins. ..." When in December the Confederates temporarily evacuated

---

[1] New Orleans *States*, January 25, 1925.
[2] Shugg, *Origins of Class Struggle in Louisiana*, 182.
[3] Minor Plantation Diary (1861-1862), October 24, 1862.
[4] Whittington (ed.), "Concerning the Loyalty of Slaves in Louisiana in 1863," *Louisiana Historical Quarterly*, XIV (October, 1931), 494.
[5] Clark, *Life in the Middle West*, 99.
[6] Minor Plantation Diary (1863-1868), September 1, 1864.

Palfrey's land, he fumed: "They have left on my plantation, devastation & desolation behind them—No discipline among them, & no regard to private property." The planter's summary on the conduct of Confederate soldiers was brief and bitter: "Our troops have stripped me, by robbery, of nearly every resource for living from day to day, & what is in reserve for me from the common enemy, is yet to be ascertained.—From a condition of ease comfort and abundance, I am suddenly reduced to one of hardship, want & privation."[1] At the time that this unqualified condemnation was written, not a Northern soldier had set foot on Palfrey's place.

Partisans and guerillas poured salt upon the wounds that planters suffered at the hands of Union and Confederate armies. Farragut's fierce reprisals against Donaldsonville and various plantation homes were brought on by partisan activities. As early as the summer of 1862, raiders were striking estates along the rivers and sniping at shipping. In August the steamboat *Sumter* was attacked while loading sugar above Bayou Sara. The mayor of the town notified the crew of their danger, and they escaped, but the steamer was burned.[2]

Guerillas were active throughout the countryside, avoiding only river and bayou towns where Federal garrisons were stationed. A Union soldier in Baton Rouge in the spring of 1863 noted that these bold raiders swarmed about the outskirts of the town, making visits by Northerners to abandoned plantations extremely hazardous.[3] When in the spring of 1863 a Bayou Teche planter went to one of his places near Opelousas, he found that the house "had been broken up & robed by the disserters—rogues who [had] long infested this neighborhood—and everything taken off...which could be moved."[4] This sugar grower preferred the stringencies of military occupation to the depredations of guerillas, and he returned to the Teche for the remainder of the war.[5] The Opelousas area was so overrun by guerillas by 1863 that Federal troops were unable to suppress them.[6]

Plantations leased from the Union army by Northern entrepreneurs

---

[1] Palfrey Plantation Diary, November 4, December 10, 19, 1862, January 22, 1863.
[2] New Orleans *Daily True Delta*, August 19, 1862.
[3] Johns, *Life with the Forty-ninth Massachusetts Volunteers*, 164.
[4] Bayside Plantation Journal, May 11, 1863.
[5] Frank L. Richardson, "War As I Saw It," *Louisiana Historical Quarterly*, VI (April, 1923), 238.
[6] Mason, *The Forty-second Ohio Infantry*, 242.

often were singled out for exceptionally severe treatment. The New Orleans *Daily True Delta* in March of 1864 declared that raiders were alarmingly active along the Mississippi between New Orleans and Donaldsonville. These marauders, asserted the editor, paid special attention to lessees of government places. "Among others," he pointed out, "they have cleaned out the plantation of Mr. Nathaniel Page, one of the correspondents of the New York *Tribune* for this department." [1] Guerillas struck in May of 1864 along the Opelousas Railroad in a sortie that admirably demonstrated their terroristic tactics. The band pounced upon a plantation leased by a Northerner, seizing four white men found on the premises. One of the captives was led a few hundred yards into the field, tied, and shot through the forehead. "This is cold-blooded murder," futilely railed a New Orleans journalist. [2]

This fierce irregular warfare was a permanent feature of the Civil War in many parts of the sugar bowl. Doubtless the editor of the New Orleans *Daily Picayune* accurately appraised these predatory despoilers in saying, "[The guerillas] do more harm to the inhabitants that yet remain upon their plantations, mostly females, than to the Federal forces." [3]

To the devastations of war in lower Louisiana were added confiscatory acts of the Union government. Acts of Congress of August 3, 1861, and July 12, 1862, authorized the confiscation of property employed in aid of the rebellion. The effectiveness of these statutes in Louisiana depended upon their implementation by General Butler. This enthusiastic officer —to Louisiana a "malignant genius"—early in the war made known his views concerning the fate of Rebel property: "Has it not been held from the beginning of the world down to this day, from the time the Israelites took possession of the land of Canaan, which they got from alien enemies—and is it not the well-settled law of war to-day that the whole property of alien enemies belonged to the conqueror, and that it is at his mercy and his clemency what should be done with it?" [4] General Butler enjoyed the work set forth for him by Congress.

On November 9, 1862, General Butler issued confiscatory General Order Number 91. This order created the District of Lafourche, which

---

[1] New Orleans *Daily True Delta*, March 26, 1864.
[2] *Ibid.*, May 31, 1864.
[3] New Orleans *Daily Picayune*, December 4, 1862.
[4] Benjamin F. Butler, *Character and Results of the War; How to Prosecute It and How to End It* (Philadelphia, 1863), 17.

included all of Louisiana west of the Mississippi River, except the parishes of Plaquemines and Jefferson. All property in the District of Lafourche was declared sequestered, all sales and transfers prohibited. A sequestration commission, composed of army officers, was to administer the order. The commission should honor claims of loyal persons and neutral foreigners. By definition, "loyal persons" were those who had not borne arms against the United States since the fall of New Orleans, who remained quietly at home, and who would "return to their allegiance" by taking a required loyalty oath.[1]

General Butler remained in command in Louisiana only two months after he issued his sequestration order. He therefore did not have an opportunity to push his policy to its limits. When in December of 1862 General Banks replaced the despised Butler, a statement was published that no further seizures of property would be made, except by specific order.[2] In the short time that General Butler was in command after the publication of General Order Number 91, the sequestration commission moved into action against the planters of lower Louisiana. An exact tabulation of the amount of goods seized on plantations is perhaps impossible, but General Butler stated that the sequestration commission "disposed of" more than $1,000,000 worth of property.[3] Plantations belonging to sugar producers prominent in Confederate civil or military affairs often were confiscated. Duncan Kenner's Ashland Plantation underwent this fate, as did Judah P. Benjamin's Belle Chasse Plantation.[4]

Sugar planters suffered crushing blows through destruction, looting, neglect of property, and confiscation. An eminent contemporary student of the sugar industry calculated these losses in equipment alone at nearly $70,000,000.[5] The editor of the New Orleans *Price-Current* scaled the figure down to $50,000,000. Actual destruction of sugarhouses and machinery probably was less than this, for the estimate counted as total loss some plants that remained of value, even though severely damaged by vandalism and neglect. Planters reckoned that the sugar industry would require a transfusion of at least $26,000,000 in

---

[1] New Orleans *Daily True Delta*, November 11, 1862.
[2] *The War of the Rebellion*, Ser. I, Vol. XV, 644.
[3] Benjamin F. Butler, *Autobiography and Personal Reminiscences of Major-General Benjamin F. Butler; Butler's Book* (Boston, 1892), 522.
[4] Work Projects Administration, *Louisiana; a Guide to the State*, 560.
[5] Latham, *Black and White*, 171.

capital to revive it; their losses from outright devastation were staggering at the least.[1]

Lower Louisiana during the Civil War presented a classic study of the ravaging of a contested area. Here was a region of America unique in its cultural and economic pattern, a section combining both agricultural and industrial enterprises under common ownership and in joint operation. The sugar country was one of the most flourishing portions of the South and was a prize more precious than rubies for the invader. Mansions and other property usually were not demolished by direct military action, as in modern war. No fleets of bombers passed over the bayou land. No battles of major proportion, except for the siege of Port Hudson, occurred there. The sugar land fell victim for an extended period to confiscations and seizures by Union authorities, to wholesale looting by the soldiery of both armies, to the unblushing vandalism of thousands of campaigners and Negroes, and to the certain ruin of abandonment and neglect. When to these blows was added the random burning of houses by vengeful Federal troops, the picture was complete. War left the cane country stricken, for the "winds of destruction" had blown from friend and foe alike.

---

[1] New Orleans *Price-Current*, September 1, 1866. Not included in this estimate of $50,000,000 was the cost of freed slaves, unharvested crops, and land depreciation.

CHAPTER VII

BARREN HARVEST

War struck the Louisiana sugar industry a crippling, almost a killing, blow. The stringencies of invasion and occupation demanded of cane planters the utmost in skill, perseverance, and craft. Anything less meant ruin. Many proprietors, lacking the strength to withstand the shock, or the pliancy to give with it, fell into defeat. Hardly more than one in seven kept going through the ordeal. General Butler's sequestration order of November 9, 1862, permitted landowners who were peaceful, and who took the oath of allegiance to the United States, to remain and work their plantations. [1] Some cane growers were sincere Unionists who welcomed the arrival of the Northern army and willingly met General Butler's requirements. Others masked their bitterness, accepted the conqueror's terms, and set about doggedly to make bricks without straw—or so they must have felt in facing their fields empty-handed.

Wartime sugar planting was beset with seemingly impossible difficulties. [2] A paralyzing stroke was the loss of mules to both Federal and Confederate armies. To cane planters of the 1860's this was a catastrophe, for a plantation of that day without livestock was comparable to a modern factory without coal or electricity. As Union forces moved up the Mississippi River and the bayous they confiscated plantation animals wholesale. [3] When the Confederates temporarily thrust back into these disputed areas, they took what was left of the worthwhile mules. The son of a prominent Terrebonne Parish producer wrote his father in 1864 that an attempt to grow a crop with the sorry teams left on the plantation was useless. [4]

---

[1] New Orleans *Daily True Delta*, November 11, 1862. Material in this chapter has been previously published in an article, "Difficulties of Civil War Sugar Planting in Louisiana," *Louisiana Historical Quarterly*, XXXVIII (October, 1955), 40-62. It is published here by courtesy of the editor of the *Louisiana Historical Quarterly*.

[2] The gravest problem facing cane producers was lack of dependable laborers. Chapter VIII deals with this aspect of wartime planting.

[3] For an account of the impressment of mules and horses by invading Federals, see Chapter VI.

[4] M. W. Minor to William J. Minor, March 21, 1864, William J. Minor and Family Papers.

The shortage of mules on plantations was regarded in some quarters as more serious even than the labor problem. A citizen of St. Mary Parish wrote despondently that the enemy had taken all of the corn and horses from places near New Iberia, and that fear of starvation was upon the people.[1] A New Orleans newspaper mirrored the sugar growers' concern that without labor and mules they would be unable to cut and grind in time to beat the deadly effects of early frost.[2] An observer traveling the river road from New Orleans to Baton Rouge caught the significance of the livestock shortage, declaring that it had left the landowners "perfectly powerless."[3]

Without mules there was no hope of growing cane, and planters spared nothing in their search for animals to keep plows and carts moving. They went day after day to nearby towns, hoping to retrieve teams taken by fleeing Negroes. Though these efforts usually were only moderately successful, proprietors managed to accumulate enough mules to keep their plantations at least in partial production. William T. Palfrey, for instance, was able in the summer of 1863 to recover a number of mules taken from his place by the invading army. He gained this concession by producing a "safeguard" that he had been resourceful and lucky enough to wangle from a local provost marshal. Even with this document, Palfrey succeeded in persuading the Union officers to return only twelve out of thirty-two animals that had been taken.[4] Other planters were forced to accept similar fractions when the Federals were in a mood to return any mules at all. Even more disheartening to landowners was the knowledge that after recovering a meager number of animals, they might expect the next formation of troops to drive off part or all of them.

The danger of having their plantations completely stripped of motive power caused owners to take unusual precautions to save what animals they could. William J. Minor in April of 1863 ordered his overseers to count and report all livestock once a week, instead of once a month as had been customary. In June he drew his regulations tighter, instructing that Negroes might use carts and wagons only by special permission.[5] The next year he attempted to guard his teams by placing them under

---

[1] Alfred C. Weeks to John Moore, January 13, 1864, David Weeks and Family Papers.
[2] New Orleans *Daily True Delta*, August 26, 1864.
[3] Hepworth, *Whip, Hoe, and Sword*, 92.
[4] Palfrey Plantation Diary, September 10, 1863.
[5] Minor Plantation Diary (1861-1865), June 12, 1863.

supervision of selected cartmen, whose sense of responsibility presumably was whetted by their being permitted to charge other laborers a fee of fifty cents a load for hauling moss into the nearby town of Houma for sale.[1]

Straitened planters were forced to substitute and improvise where possible and to wring maximum use out of the scant remaining mule supply. Oxen sometimes took over the tasks of absent mules. In May of 1863 Governor Thomas O. Moore received word from another Rapides Parish planter that among many efforts being made to grow sugar was the employment of oxen at the plows.[2] During the grinding season of 1864 William T. Palfrey's carts of fresh-cut cane bumped laboriously toward the sugarhouse behind teams of these outmoded beasts.[3] In an informal way producers pooled their mule resources by lending and borrowing among themselves. Palfrey's operations during the 1864-1865 grinding season demonstrated this expediency. On November 23, 1864, he began cutting cane on his Bayou Cypre Mort place, using four mules and two pairs of oxen borrowed from a neighbor.[4] The next day he was able to get ten mules from another friend to assist in sugar making. Four days later another acquaintance sent Palfrey four mules, and early in December the planter borrowed three additional mules from a cooperative neighbor.[5]

In the early years of the war, losses of mules were irreplaceable, since Louisiana was isolated from sources of supply in Missouri, Tennessee, and Kentucky. By 1864 the success of Union arms in the West had re-established transportation among these states, and shipments of mules again were arriving in the cane country. Prices were high, but to those who could scrape up money or credit, mules were cheap at any cost, for they were indispensable. Planters were able in April of 1864 to buy animals at over $200 each, as advertisements in New Orleans newspapers marked frequent arrivals from states farther north.[6] The Varieties Stables in New Orleans received numerous shipments of mules destined for the cane fields, announcing in March of 1864, for example, a sale of 200

---

[1] *Ibid.*, October 8, 1864.
[2] Whittington (ed.), "Concerning the Loyalty of Slaves in Louisiana in 1863," *Louisiana Historical Quarterly*, XIV (October, 1931), 494.
[3] Palfrey Plantation Diary, November 17, 1864.
[4] *Ibid.*, November 23, 1864.
[5] *Ibid.*, November 28, December 3, 1864.
[6] Minor Plantation Diary (1863-1868), April 24, 1864.

good animals from Missouri and Kentucky.[1] In December Dr. P. Halpin of New Orleans called attention to his sale of fifty young Kentucky mules "with a good title"—a descriptive phrase suggesting that not everybody in those troubled days was careful as to whose livestock he peddled.[2]

The sale by the United States army of condemned animals frequently increased plantation supply. Planters sometimes purchased mules— unwittingly one may suppose—stolen from the Federals. In any case, this cast-off government stock was not the most desirable, and in the fall of 1865 a salesman announcing 400 Kentucky mules, "green and broke," was cautious to point out that no government animals were among them.[3] Though from time to time proprietors were able to replenish their livestock resources, the supply was meager and unpredictable. Many landowners found the price above reach, and a shortage of mules plagued sugar planters until the end of the war and beyond.

The exigencies of war caused many sugar growers to diversify their planting. Production of cotton, corn, and sometimes tobacco required fewer laborers and mules and less capital than did the cultivation of sugar. This was a cogent argument to men desperately short of all of these assets. Most sugar producers early in the conflict substantially increased their planting of corn in order to strengthen the food supply of the Confederacy. By the time the Northern army reached the bayou country the abundance of corn was such as to stir frequent comment among observant campaigners. A young Federal officer in 1863 recorded that fields near Opelousas customarily planted in cane were then filled with corn.[4] Another invader, traversing the western portion of the sugar land and passing for miles through immense fields of luxuriant corn, took wry amusement from the "ponderous articles" of Northern newspapers that harped on the simplicity of starving the South into submission.[5]

Many planters despaired of sugar and turned to cotton, a transition sparked in 1864 by a severe shortage of seed cane. By June most of the

---

[1] New Orleans *Times*, March 13, 1864.
[2] *Ibid.*, December 28, 1864.
[3] *Ibid.*, October 1, 1865.
[4] L. Carroll Root (ed.), "Private Journal of William H. Root, Second Lieutenant, Seventy-fifth New York Volunteers, April 1-June 14, 1863," introduction by Walter Prichard, *Louisiana Historical Quarterly*, XIX (July, 1936), 651.
[5] George W. Powers, *The Story of the Thirty-eighth Massachusetts Volunteers* (Cambridge, 1866), 83.

plantations of lower Louisiana were planted in one third cane, one third corn, and one third cotton. Commenting that the sugar cane generally looked good that year, a Plaquemines Parish correspondent of the New Orleans *Daily True Delta* ruefully noted that the greater part of the land in his parish was in cotton.[1] Landowners who went over to cotton sometimes had to improvise equipment to cultivate and harvest it. One Bayou Teche proprietor, having no bagging material, resorted to compressing his cotton into sugar hogsheads, but after working an entire day at the experiment he was able to get only about 300 pounds into a hogshead and concluded that the result was not worth the effort.[2] Another producer met the shortage of cloth for cotton-picking sacks by having his laborers fashion baskets to contain the cotton.[3]

Attempts to prosper by turning from cane to cotton ended in failure. The climate of lower Louisiana had never favored the growing of cotton, and years before the Civil War planters had abandoned it for sugar. In addition to the normal handicap of inhospitable climate in the bayou country, the cotton crop of 1864 in that area was beset by drought and pests. Ruin was the result. As early as May William J. Minor lamented that his cotton was wretched, with little of it up and none of it even a "tolerable stand." In October his story was finished, as he wrote dejectedly that almost his entire cotton crop had been picked and ginned in a day, and that the whole amounted to only about five or six bales.[4]

The experience of the Pughs of the Bayou Lafourche region brought into high relief the general misfortune of those who sought escape in planting cotton. In July A. Franklin Pugh, upon hearing a report that caterpillars were stripping the cotton near Donaldsonville at the head of the bayou, predicted ruin for the entire crop if the pests should spread. His fears had foundation, for the caterpillars attacked crops throughout the state. In September Pugh recorded that his cotton had been picked twice and that he supposed only about 12,000 pounds of seed cotton had been gathered, with about an equal amount yet in the fields. "And this from over 600 acres....," he groaned. "A miserable yield, I shall not pay expenses." A month later Pugh observed dolefully that the cotton crop was a complete loss along the Lafourche, and that some

---

[1] New Orleans *Daily True Delta*, June 11, 1864.
[2] Bayside Plantation Journal, April 8, 1863.
[3] Minor Plantation Diary (1863-1868), May 25, 1864.
[4] *Ibid.*, May 23, October 22, 1864.

plantations had made neither cotton nor corn.[1] The editor of the New Orleans *Daily True Delta* penned a glum epitaph for the 1864 cotton crop in the cane land, saying that it had succumbed to the twin forces of unfavorable weather and caterpillars.[2]

Wartime stress often overtaxed relations between proprietors and overseers who remained on the plantations. In April of 1862 the Confederate States Congress passed an act conscripting white men, with certain exceptions, between the ages of eighteen and thirty-five. Fearing to strip the black belts of all white men, Congress permitted the owner or overseer to remain on each plantation of twenty Negroes. This did not relieve the shortage of overseers, as many of them volunteered into the Confederate army, and frequently landowners supervised estates in person.[3]

The vexations of dealing with unruly Negroes under Federal military occupation were too great for the manager of Magnolia Plantation. In the fall of 1862 he temporarily resigned, and the owner noted regretfully that his subaltern was too delicate to remain in charge. After paying him in full, the employer offered him, in consideration of past faithfulness, a home on the plantation as long as he should choose to remain.[4]

William T. Palfrey also had trouble in this quarter. In September of 1862 he dismissed his overseer with the curt remark that the man had been of no use to him for the last two months. After serving as his own overseer for several weeks Palfrey was able to hire a new manager for $100 a month.[5]

William J. Minor underwent exceptionally serious overseer difficulties growing out of the nature of the times. His gravest altercation was with Ewing Chapman, overseer of Hollywood Plantation. In the fall of 1863 Minor wrathfully discharged Chapman in the climax of a long series of incidents that gradually brought the planter to explosion. Minor penned a remark in the spring of the year that disclosed a growing friction. In changing certain regulations in connection with plantation procedure, the planter observed sarcastically, "Mr. Chapman does not approve of

---

[1] Barnes F. Lathrop, "The Pugh Plantations, 1860-1865; a Study of Life in Lower Louisiana" (Unpublished Ph.D. Dissertation, University of Texas, Austin, 1945), 345-362, *passim.*
[2] New Orleans *Daily True Delta*, October 1, 1864.
[3] Shugg, *Origins of Class Struggle in Louisiana*, 176.
[4] Magnolia Plantation Journal, September 3, 1862.
[5] Palfrey Plantation Diary, September 12, November 11, 1862.

this way of working, but as he is a crack overseer I don't expect he will approve of any thing that he does not suggest himself." Sources of resentment continued to accumulate. In August the owner complained that the overseer had had but little fodder pulled, notwithstanding the fact that unmistakable orders had been issued for this to be done. Chapman greatly irritated his employer by building a bridge across a small bayou on the plantation—against the planter's wishes and advice. By late summer the sugar producer reached the conclusion that his overseer was slack in taking care of the Negroes.[1]

A short time later Minor discovered that the disturbing manager had shipped sugar and molasses to his family in New Orleans, without taking the trouble to pay for the goods, and that he had upset discipline among the workers by telling them that they were free and should act accordingly. The employer suspected that Chapman had been responsible for having the Confederate army, during a raid into the Bayou Lafourche area, to hang one of the plantation Negroes.

What aroused the proprietor to towering fury was his subordinate's incessant tattling to both Federal and Confederate troops. The planter was Unionist in sympathy, but the vagaries of war in his section of the state forced landowners for self-preservation to trim to the military pattern of the moment. When the Union army overran the plantation the overseer painted the owner as a Rebel, and when in the summer of 1863 General Richard Taylor's Confederates surged for a time back into the lower sugar parishes, Chapman told the Southerners that Minor was, to borrow from the planter's prudish pen, a "d - n Yankee." After the Federals moved back into Terrebonne Parish on the heels of Taylor's retreating troops, Chapman again ran to them with his stories, accusing Minor of interfering with the management of the Negroes in such a way as to discourage their working.

Minor finally severed his connection with the overseer, whom he thoroughly despised, but he was unable to purge his thoughts of the episode. Days after the dismissal he returned to his literary attack, charging in his diary that the overseer had demoralized the Negroes as much as an abolitionist, and storming that Chapman and his two sons were three of the most unprincipled men of his entire acquaintance.[2]

Arresting side issues often accompanied the planters' search for overseers and sugar makers. One cane producer resolved to hire a Federal

---

[1] Minor Plantation Diary (1863), January 3, April 25, August 11.
[2] Minor Plantation Diary (1863-1868), October 5, 8, 1863.

soldier to serve as guard and overseer, for he had decided that only a man in uniform would be able to make the laborers turn out at daylight, do a reasonable day's work, and remain in the hospital day and night when sick or feigning sickness.[1] A landowner advertising for a sober, honest, and preferably German nightwatchman at a salary of twelve dollars a month promised a bonus of eight dollars if the man's wife were a handy gardener.[2]

The change from slave to hired labor brought a shift in emphasis in employing overseers. The old discipline was gone; tact and the threat of docking wages replaced whip and stocks. The new situation was reflected in a search by planters for employees who knew the etiquette of dealing with wage laborers. Proprietors began to seek overseers who had had experience in the new order, or who felt that they could adjust to it. Overseers seeking employment stressed past success in dealing with free laborers. A recent immigrant from the West Indies, for example, in attempting to find a position on a sugar plantation would announce that he had worked with hired laborers for years.[3]

The presence of the Federal army often galled people of the cane country, and proprietors frequently complained of interference in one form or other. The experiences of William T. Palfrey, who had numerous minor but irritating brushes with the invaders, demonstrated some of the sources of friction. In the winter of 1864—to mention an interesting incident—Palfrey was forbidden by Union authorities to visit his Bayou Cypre Mort plantation. Feeling that his presence was badly needed on the plantation, Palfrey determined to disobey the order, and on February 27 he fell in with a long train of Northern army wagons moving out of Franklin on Bayou Teche in the direction of the Bayou Cypre Mort place. He supposed that the Federals were making a corn-foraging expedition. The enemy cavalry espied Palfrey as he rode behind their column and drove him away, but the resourceful planter took to bypaths unknown to the Northern campaigners, outdistanced them by a circuitous route, inspected his land, and returned to Franklin, having ridden fifty-one miles during the day.[4] The hardships of war had not cut the vigor of this sixty-one-year-old sugar planter.

Local provost marshals at that time played a role similar to that of

---

[1] *Ibid.*, June 12, 1863.
[2] New Orleans *Times*, April 19, 1864.
[3] *Ibid.*, March 26, 1865.
[4] Palfrey Plantation Diary, February 27, 1864.

military government officers in modern war. They held power to destroy planters, controlling the labor supply and sometimes exercising judicial functions in plantation affairs, to the extreme annoyance of the owners. The case of a St. James Parish cane grower illustrated the arbitrary use of authority by one of these officials. In December of 1863 the provost marshal of the parish informed the proprietor that a man had sworn that forty hogsheads of sugar on the landowner's place belonged to him. The planter was to hold the disputed sugar, awaiting a decision of the provost marshal, or show proof that the claimant was in error.[1] On another occasion a provost marshal peremptorily ordered the same planter to pay a man and woman a debt that they alleged he owed them, or failing to pay, he was to appear before the Federal official to settle the matter.[2] Cane growers who were incensed by such minor interferences lacked the perspective to see that the provost marshals did them invaluable service in keeping the Negroes reasonably well in line on the plantations.

Cane country homes did not provide sanctuary from the intrusion of Northern soldiers, who frequently entered in search of spies and guerillas, or on one pretext or another. An incident on the Lafourche in the fall of 1862 demonstrated this violability. A detachment of Federals visited a home in Donaldsonville in an effort to capture the owner, who was believed to be the leader of a band of troublesome guerillas. The troops reached the house late at night and stationed themselves at strategic points about the premises to head off escape. The officer in charge then led a party into the house, to find it occupied by only three women and a young boy. A "buxom" young widow, who made no mean impression on the searchers, informed them that the owner was her cousin. She asserted that he was not a guerilla, that he was not at home, and that the Federals were at liberty to search at their pleasure. Unable to arrest the absent owner, or to discover any hidden weapons, and perhaps determined not to return empty-handed to his superiors, the leader of the group called for the overseer, and that unfortunate individual was forced to accompany the Union detachment as a prisoner.[3]

---

[1] Henry D. Pope to Andrew E. Crane, December 20, 1863, Andrew E. Crane Papers (Department of Archives, Louisiana State University, Baton Rouge).
[2] J. D. Rich to Andrew E. Crane, May 3, 1865, Andrew E. Crane Papers.
[3] George G. Smith, *Leaves from a Soldier's Diary; the Personal Record of Lieutenant George G. Smith, First Louisiana Regiment Infantry Volunteers* (Putnam, Connecticut, 1906), 32-33.

By 1864 the sugar industry faced extinction from a severe shortage of seed cane. Many planters, despondent over the chaotic state of their plantations, and not knowing from one season to the next whether there would be another crop, sent to the mill the cane that customarily would have been saved for planting. General Banks saw the danger and moved to stop proprietors from grinding all of the meager 1864-1865 harvest. His General Order Number 138, issued September 22, 1864, provided that all owners, lessees, and managers of sugar plantations should reserve one fourth of the season's yield as seed cane. In case of sale or transfer of a plantation, the seller should receive credit for his seed cane at market value. [1]

The effect of Banks' order is indeterminable, for to all men it was all things. Friends of the Federals saw in it the salvation of sugar in Louisiana, while a New Orleans editor averred icily that the order contained nothing new and scoffed at the suggestion that without it the industry would have perished. [2] Whether sugar growers would have saved seed cane without being prodded by military authority is debatable. That an encouraging quantity of seed cane was saved is beyond cavil, for producers even turned from grinding to selling seed cane in order to profit from their 1864-1865 crop. Advertisements in newspapers calling attention to the sale of seed cane, usually in "mattresses," were testimony to its existence. William J. Minor, in an effort to save as much as possible, put down eighty per cent of his crop for this purpose. [3] By February of 1865 the shortage of seed cane had eased noticeably. A New Orleans newspaper advised its readers in florid lines that no longer was there danger of the disappearance of sugar from lower Louisiana; that ample seed cane had been saved, and that it only required planting and care "to ripen into the fullness of a heavy crop, and crown the hopes of the trusting agriculturalist with a bounteous harvest." [4]

Deterioration of the levees was a cause of grave concern to sugar cultivators along the Mississippi River. Each landowner before the war customarily maintained that section of the levee along his own front. This was now impossible, and in many places the earthen barriers had dissolved before the force of the river. As early as June of 1862 William J. Minor received information from his son that Waterloo Plantation

---

[1] New Orleans *Daily True Delta*, September 18, 1864.
[2] *Ibid.*, February 11, 1865.
[3] Minor Plantation Diary (1863-1868), October 25, 1864.
[4] New Orleans *Daily True Delta*, February 10, 1865.

was in danger of being inundated, that much of the land already was flooded, and that the Negroes were living in temporary shanties to escape high water, which had driven them from their quarters.[1] Confederate and guerilla forces increased the problem of flood control, often cutting levees, either to hamper Union military operations or to drive out government lessees and collaborating planters.[2] Federal authorities attempted to maintain the levees by issuing orders that proprietors should comply with existing parish laws providing for their upkeep.[3] This was unrealistic and futile, as many plantations were abandoned and idle, and before the end of the war a large portion of the most fertile land in the cane country was rendered unproductive by overflow.[4]

Inhabitants of the cane land knew intimately the rigors of war, as food, clothing, medicine, and plantation supplies grew scarce, and prices soared. In the spring of 1862 a large Terrebonne Parish planter began to feel the pinch, as his slaves were in critical want of pork, shoes, and clothing.[5] An English traveler in the state tabulated the skyrocketing prices of commodities purchased by Louisiana citizens in clandestine trade with Northerners—$130 for a sack of salt; 75 cents a pound for bacon and hams, a high figure by standards of the time; and $20 an ounce for quinine.[6] Rare items grew increasingly expensive, if not unobtainable at any cost. In August of 1862 A. Franklin Pugh, a fancier of good cigars, glumly scrawled in the margin of his diary that he had smoked his last.[7] By April of 1864 quinine in New Iberia was selling for $100 an ounce.[8]

Women were perhaps harder hit by many of the war shortages than were men. To them the lack of books, new gowns, coffee, loaf sugar, and lemons—to mention a few items for which one plantation matron longed—was a telling blow. Bolted cornmeal substituted for flour in

---

[1] Minor Plantation Diary (1861-1862), June 14, 1862.
[2] Nathaniel P. Banks, *Emancipated Labor in Louisiana* (New York, 1864), 12.
[3] New Orleans *Daily True Delta*, October 24, 1862.
[4] *De Bow's Review*, III, N.S. (April and May, 1867), 469-473, *passim*.
[5] J. Carlyle Sitterson, "The McCollams; a Planter Family of the Old and New South," *Journal of Southern History*, VI (August, 1940), 359.
[6] W. C. Corsan, *Two Months in the Confederate States; Including a Visit to New Orleans under the Domination of General Butler* (London, 1863), 65.
[7] Pugh Plantation Diary, August 1, 1862.
[8] John A. Smith to "Sir" [John Moore], April 24, 1864, David Weeks and Family Papers.

making cakes, and the abundance of open-kettle brown sugar enabled Louisiana folk to prepare ample quantities of crude candies and other sweets.[1] A young Baton Rouge girl, who spent several months as a refugee on a sugar plantation, and who recalled wistfully the many delicacies that she had once considered necessities, even tried hailstones in her hunger for ice. Bread she had believed essential to life, and vegetables useless, she wrote, but she had been forced to get along without bread and to cultivate a toleration for vegetables.[2]

The word "Confederate" took on new meaning in the vocabulary of austerity. As an adjective it meant crude, unfashionable, or obsolete. Confederate dresses were old and out-moded; a Confederate bridle was a rope halter; Confederate silver was tin cups and spoons; and Confederate flour was rough cornmeal. Young ladies of the sugar plantations rode to military dress parades at nearby Port Hudson, Louisiana, in Confederate carriages—rough wagons fitted with seats, covered with leather stretched over hickory laths, and drawn by mules.[3]

Medical supplies on the plantations were inadequate, and disease struck planters' families and slaves with extraordinary effect. Quinine shortages made malaria a graver menace than usual, while scanty clothing and fuel invited colds and pneumonia. Measles, whooping cough, and typhoid fever raced through the plantation communities. In October of 1862 fever of an undisclosed variety spread among the Negroes on a St. Mary Parish estate and brought work to a standstill.[4] Typhoid fever during the summer of 1864 laid William T. Palfrey's workers low. Many died of it, and in October the owner himself came down with the dread disease, from which he painfully recovered.[5] Diphtheria appeared in Rapides Parish in the spring of 1863, taking heavy toll among the children of some places. A plantation inhabitant recommended to his wife a fearful remedy that involved smearing the patient all over with lard and administering heavy doses of calomel twice a day. "But if such a disease should get on the place send for a doctor...., he wisely urged. "God forbid that any such should get amongst us." In an effort to economize, the same individual planned to

---

[1] Merrick, *Old Times in Dixie Land*, 59.
[2] Dawson, *A Confederate Girl's Diary*, 224.
[3] *Ibid.*, 233.
[4] I. A. Johnson to John Moore, October 14, 1862, David Weeks and Family Papers.
[5] Palfrey Plantation Diary, October 15, 1864.

have his children vaccinated against smallpox and to save the scabs for use in immunizing the Negro children.[1]

Lacking a market for their sugar, planters racked their brains for ways to gain profit on the blockaded produce. One Rapides Parish landowner had the ingenuity to dispose of his crop by converting it into rum. In March of 1863 he sold a large quantity of this homemade beverage for $17,000. Stored in Alexandria he had another 100 barrels of the fiery liquid, estimated to be worth $40,000.[2] Another sugar producer was disquieted upon finding that one of his Negroes was diverting sugar from what the planter felt was its true mission; the resourceful black had rigged a still on the plantation and was turning out rum.[3]

Invasion of the cane country gave Federal soldiers an opportunity to look into the interior of one food industry long before the day of pure food laws. A fastidious Northerner, who might have written a Civil War prototype of Upton Sinclair's shocking revelation of filth in food preparation, did not like what he saw in the sugarhouses. From Plaquemine, Louisiana, he sent home this revolting and perhaps exaggerated description of wartime sugar making: "... I think the process just about the nastiest affair I have anywhere witnessed. I will never again be able to take a spoonful of sugar-house molasses without thinking 'rat' and having visions of extract of the filthy creatures floating through my memory, as I found them floating through the sweet mass; the living, struggling and crawling over the dead and dying animals. You may charge me with bad taste in trying to deprive you of a pleasure in the future.... If, however, you want to 'lick 'lasses and swing on a gate,' go it whilst you are young, but if you live ... to see just such sights as I have seen you will 'look twice before you leap.' "[4]

The war smashed banks and firms of commission merchants in the cane country, as well as plantations, leaving proprietors caught with no sources of credit. Moneylenders could lend no funds until planters paid their debts; planters could not meet their obligations as long as they could grow no sugar; and plantations could not produce sugar

---

[1] Robert Newell to Sarah Ann Newell, March 31, 1863, Robert Newell and Family Papers (Department of Archives, Louisiana State University).
[2] *Ibid.*, March ?, 1863.
[3] Minor Plantation Diary (1863-1868), January 14, 1865.
[4] Benjamin Franklin Stevenson, *Letters from the Army* (Cincinnati, 1884), 282-283.

without being rehabilitated—a costly process.¹ With their economic stroke caught at dead center, distraught sugar growers became practitioners of a calculated realism in attempting to regain motion. Two methods promised relief. Cultivators fraternized with Federal provost marshals and other officials, hoping to gain favors of one kind or another, and they often leased their plantations or formed partnerships with men of money and influence—usually Northerners—who hoped to find quick fortune in the cane fields.

Friendship with a provost marshal might pay off handsomely in assisting a proprietor to keep discipline among his laborers. In July of 1862 workers on an estate near Donaldsonville refused to go into the fields. A steamboat shortly swung in to the wharf, and a formation of Union troops disembarked and filed toward the Negro quarter. The officer in command met expostulations of the laborers with the curt statement that he was there to maintain order, not to redress grievances. Then, amidst mutterings that "dis is more worser dan Jeff Davis," he placed the leading agitators in stocks.² Relations between the owner of the plantation and the local provost marshal obviously were quite cordial. From time to time when laborers on his plantations grew rebellious, William J. Minor called upon Northern soldiers to intimidate them into returning to work. In the fall of 1863 a number of Federal officers who dined with Minor told him of disciplinary action that they had taken that day with Negroes on the Duncan Kenner place. The officers had searched the quarter for stolen sugar, and having discovered fifteen barrels hidden away, they had seized the laborers' corn as payment for the goods.³ In November Minor reported to the local provost marshal the theft of a cart and team by one of his blacks. This official called in the Negro, tried him, and sentenced him to confinement in jail at night on bread and water. During the daytime the culprit was to work under guard on the levee.⁴

Proprietors sometimes were able to persuade Federal commanders to station troops more or less permanently on their premises to keep unmanageable Negroes in line. A Northern soldier described with a dash of irony one of these planters, a Terrebonne Parish landowner

---

[1] The New Orleans *Daily True Delta*, February 10, 1865, carried a cogent analysis of the interaction of lending agencies and plantations in the economic stagnation of the war years.

[2] Watson, *Life in the Confederate Army*, 398.

[3] Minor Plantation Diary (1863), August 18, September 7.

[4] Minor Plantation Diary (1863-1868), November 24, 1863.

who was nominally loyal to the Union, though one of his sons was in the Confederate army. The cane grower was a frequent visitor in the Federal encampment, where he ingratiated himself with the commander and prevailed upon him to order a small detachment of troops to remain on his plantation to act as referees between the overseer and the laborers. This plan kept the blacks at work, while the soldiers lived in the owner's house, hunted, fished, and "had a jolly time." [1]

The belief grew in some quarters that provost marshals no longer shielded the Negroes, but that these officers had fallen under the domination of planters, becoming tyrants instead of protectors. A highly literate Northern campaigner applied his scathing pen to this alliance between occupation officials and landowners: "My courteous Captain [previously a violent abolitionist] presently takes unto himself pleasant relationships with much-abused planters, and with widowed proprietresses of elegant mansions and sugar estates, and with ladies whose husbands and brothers are rebel generals, colonels, and the like; whereafter all awkward Northern prejudices concerning Southern institutions are gracefully waived in deference to that 'good society' into which our provost-captain is post-prandially inducted, and the quondam 'abolitionist' becomes 'votre très humble serviteur' to all the creole barons and baronesses who choose to smile on him." [2]

Leasing plantations and forming partnerships, frequently with Northerners, lightened the onerous burdens of wartime planting. Throughout the struggle newspapers bore notices of establishments for rent or lease—advertisements usually framed like this: "For lease—A plantation in Lafourche Parish, containing 1200 acres of Cleared Land, 75 of which is now being planted in Cane, with all the necessary utensils for working the same—Mules, Carts, Corn, Hay, etc. Sugar-House and Engine in running order." [3] Effingham Lawrence of Magnolia Plantation below New Orleans was one of the first to see the possibilities of this plan, and he leased his place in September of 1862 to a man with sufficient capital to operate it. [4]

Other owners preferred to bring in partners, hoping that they might attract men whose wealth and connections would offset their own

---

[1] Marshall, *Army Life; from a Soldier's Journal*, 337.
[2] Duganne, *Camps and Prisons*, 43. For additional evidence on this point, see Charles Kassel, *The Labor System of General Banks; a Lost Episode of Civil War History* (n.p., n.d.), 45.
[3] New Orleans *Times*, November 14, 1864.
[4] Magnolia Plantation Journal, January 25, 1863.

humiliating poverty and helplessness. The terms of these liaisons varied from place to place, but the central thought was to form a combination in which one party supplied the means of cultivating land belonging to the other. A few examples revealed the process. The wife of one of the most distinguished planters of Iberville Parish in January of 1864 engaged a partner to take over a plantation. He was to put up one third of the capital to operate the place a year and in return was to receive one third of the net profit from the year's crop.[1] A St. James Parish sugar producer formed a partnership with an entrepreneur in order to obtain money to make a crop. The contract required the landowner to provide land, buildings, stables, Negro cabins, machinery, tools, and wood to produce sugar. The partner was to put up money for wages and supply seventeen pounds of pork per worker each month. Profit would be equally shared.[2] A Terrebonne Parish planter agreed to let two businessmen have an interest in his sugar crop. They were to provide laborers and to receive one half of the year's output of sugar.[3]

One senses from a letter written by William J. Minor's son the air of intrigue that hung over the sugar land during the war. Young Minor asked his father for instructions and made his own suggestions for improving the grave condition of Waterloo Plantation. Summing up the hardships of trying to make sugar without adequate teams, while plagued with indolent Negroes and poor seed cane, young Minor implored, "Authorize me to rent and I will take in a partner who has and will continue to have influence over the hands (and in other places) and I will take care of the *outside* affairs...."[4] Precisely what he meant by "outside affairs" does not appear, but the reference to someone of influence is transparent.

The wartime tribulations of sugar planters defied solution. Minor wrote dejectedly that he was not equal to the task, and that if it were not for his wife and children he would be tempted to turn everything loose and to flee until the war was over. No sooner was one trying

---

[1] Contract between Emily J. Randolph and W. I. Brown, January 4, 1864, John Hampden Randolph and Family Papers (Department of Archives, Louisiana State University).

[2] Contract between Andrew E. Crane and C. R. Kunemann, January 26, 1864, Andrew E. Crane Papers.

[3] Minor Plantation Diary (1863-1868), October 29, 1864.

[4] M. W. Minor to William J. Minor, March 21, 1864, William J. Minor and Family Papers.

problem solved than another rose in its place. "I act for the best," he brooded. "But I act blindly—I am in the dark."[1] Minor was not alone in the blackness. Sugar plantations fell idle by hundreds, and in 1865 less than 200 of these once prosperous establishments bore even a token crop. Planters of the stricken cane country reflected with nostalgia on the days of peace and plenty before the war.

---

[1] Minor Plantation Diary (1863), February 26.

CHAPTER VIII

EMANCIPATED LABOR

The supreme social and economic result of war in the cane country was the freeing of the area's 139,000 Negro slaves, an action that transformed a great mass of black humanity from chattels into citizens. Of greater immediate concern to sugar growers was the fact that it drastically upset for many years the plantation labor system and left owners virtually helpless. Out of the confusion of war rose many of the racial problems that would crystallize in the period of reconstruction and remain to plague generations of Southerners, both black and white, even to the present. Planters effectively held in line the multitude of slaves on sugar plantations during the months of faraway war before Union forces invaded the cane land. Rigid pass laws and alert patrols insured decorum among the blacks, and no attempt to rebel or flee the plantations in large numbers occurred before the arrival of Northern troops.

The coming of the Federal army changed overnight this docility and quickened in the slaves a latent urge to escape. Many laborers harbored a deep longing for freedom, and they had for months been aware that a war was raging that would deeply affect their future. Sensing that the blue-clad Northern soldiers were liberators, they flocked to Federal encampments and left the cane fields unattended. In the words of one writer, the movement of a Union column into the cane land stirred swarms of laborers, "like thrusting a walking-stick into an ant-hill...." [1] Before the capture of New Orleans the invaders attracted the Negroes of plantations along the Mississippi River below the city. In early April of 1862 the overseer of Magnolia Plantation frequently scrawled into the plantation journal his semi-literate complaints that workers were slipping away to the "Lincolnits" at Fort Jackson; that "there [were] a good many negroes Leving and going to the enemy."

Compounded with an impulse for freedom was a strong element of childlike curiosity that motivated the Negroes to sally out to meet the Northerners. They were interested in seeing what manner of men these much-heralded Yankees really were, and they often were disappointed,

---

[1] James Parton, *General Butler in New Orleans; Being a History of the Administration of the Department of the Gulf in the Year 1862* (New York, 1864), 489.

for runaways began in May to drift back to the plantations. Those returning to Magnolia Plantation from Fort Jackson and Fort St. Philip declared that they had "Seen the Eliphant" and were happy to be home.

Planters realized keenly that a disruption of their labor by the presence of the Union army would be ruinous if not quickly curbed, and they took immediate steps to retrieve as many runaways as possible before crops deteriorated beyond remedy. These efforts during the early stages of the invasion usually were successful. The Magnolia Plantation overseer applied on June 14 to Northern authorities at the forts for permission to collect his workers and take them back to their cabins. The Federal commander, doubtless happy to be rid of the responsibility of providing for great numbers of indolent blacks, gave consent.[1] Many other plantation managers were at the forts on similar missions, and they probably met with equal success.

During the summer of 1862 the Negroes of parishes below New Orleans grew increasingly restive. Owners were unable to maintain discipline among workers because of the nearness of protecting Federal troops—an advantage not lost on the blacks. Large gangs of plantation Negroes wandered almost at will into New Orleans and the Union army camps, seeking freedom, excitement, and escape from toil. Newspapers of the city abounded in accounts of these unorganized invasions by groups of unruly laborers. "This morning, about five o'clock," recorded the New Orleans *Daily True Delta*, "another gang of contrabands came up to the city from the lower coast, and succeeded in reaching the Customshouse or some other place of refuge."[2] New Orleans by fall of 1862 was host to about 10,000 vagrant blacks, while other throngs were accumulated at Fort Jackson and Fort St. Philip below the city, and at Camp Parapet on the river above.[3]

As Federal authority spread up the Mississippi River, the problem of runaway Negroes moved with it. After the capture of Baton Rouge laborers crowded in from the sugar plantations that lay in every direction around the capital city. Desire for freedom and excitement at least temporarily overpowered the maternal instinct of some Negro mothers, for the mistress of a nearby sugar estate wrote in amazement, "Several women, in their eagerness, and desiring to be unencumbered, left their

---

[1] Magnolia Plantation Journal, May 7, 30, June 14, 1862.
[2] New Orleans *Daily True Delta*, August 6, 1862.
[3] Parton, *General Butler in New Orleans*, 522.

sleeping babies in the cabin beds." Yielding to this show of loyalty and confidence on the part of the slaves, the Federals shipped them to New Orleans for sanctuary.[1] A Northern soldier, astonished at the dark tidal wave that swept over the city, recorded: "The only thing that is low [in price] at Baton Rouge is the 'Contrabands,' these are plenty at a low figure. They swarm in, whole plantations at a time."[2]

General Godfrey Weitzel's invasion of the Bayou Lafourche sugar country in October of 1862 cut the bonds of additional thousands of plantation slaves, and they lost no time in taking flight from their masters. The change that came over the Negroes at the approach of Union forces was immediate and obvious. After Weitzel's troops pushed by one plantation, the mistress assembled her laborers for an admonitory talk. She was dismayed at the transition. "They came slowly and reluctantly," she recalled. "I see before me now those dark stolid faces in which I read nothing—I was among a strange people, and was unprepared for a change so great—I looked vainly in familiar faces for the old expression—they listened attentively, there was no response, not a sound—it was ominous in so excitable a people." The next morning this woman awakened to a plantation deserted by the freedom-seeking blacks. Only a few old or sick ones remained.[3]

During the next few weeks the Bayou Lafourche labor force melted away rapidly. On October 28 a great planter noted that his workers were restive and "in a bad way." Two days later they were "completely demoralized," as the owner expressed it, and leaving the place in carts. By November nearly all were gone from two of the plantations that this proprietor ran, and on the third of the month only 31 out of 100 Negroes remained on another of his places.[4] The great exodus from the Lafourche was accomplished.

General Weitzel was sorely plagued by the hordes of Negroes that gathered about his brigade. In consternation he wrote to General Butler: "What shall I do about the negroes? You can form no idea of the vicinity of my camp, nor can you form an idea of the appearance of my brigade as it marched down the bayou. My train was larger than any army train

---

[1] Ripley, *From Flag to Flag*, 46.
[2] Lloyd (ed.), *A Memorial of Lieutenant Daniel Perkins Dewey, of the Twenty-fifth Regiment, Connecticut Volunteers*, 48.
[3] Lathrop, "The Pugh Plantations, 1860-1865; a Study of Life in Lower Louisiana," 209.
[4] Pugh Plantation Diary, November 3, 1862.

for 25,000 men. Every soldier had a negro marching in the flanks, carrying his knapsack. Plantation carts, filled with negro women and children, with their effects; and of course compelled to pillage for their subsistence, as I have no rations to issue them. I have a great many more negroes in my camp now than I have whites.... These negroes are a perfect nuisance." [1]

The first Northern sweep up Bayou Teche set adrift other multitudes of Negroes. William T. Palfrey on November 3, 1862, hurried his slaves into the swamp behind the cane fields because he feared that the shot from Federal gunboats might fall among them. A few days later he moved them and their "things" to his Bayou Cypre Mort plantation, where he believed they would be safer from invaders. In May Palfrey described the mass movement of workers from the western rim of the sugar land as "An enormous train of about 8000 negroes in carts & waggons escorted by about 2000 of the enemy's troops [who] passed through our Parish this day, bound for Berwick's Bay." The planter indignantly charged that this host of slaves had been stolen or enticed away from their rightful owners in the western parishes. [2]

The behavior of the Negroes in the northern sugar areas was no exception to the general story of desertion as the Union army approached. When in 1863 the Northern spearhead drove into the Red River Valley, it attracted vast numbers of blacks just as it had done in the lower parishes. An Alexandria journalist accused the Northerners of sowing seeds of dissatisfaction and insurrection among the laborers. Over 3,000 Negroes fled from Rapides Parish as the Federals withdrew. "Almost every planter has lost some [slaves] and a few lost all," the editor stated furiously. "The deluded wretches were hurried off and a thousand stories poured into their bewildering ears...." [3]

This habit of the blacks of running away to the Northern army was a feature of plantation life to the end of the war. Workers often returned to masters, but their stay was always precarious, for they might at any moment and on the slightest whim leave for the nearest Union camp. Evidence selected at random illustrated the state of flux in which labor affairs remained throughout the conflict. On September 1, 1863, the New Orleans *Daily True Delta* referred to the situation around Baton

---

[1] Parton, *General Butler in New Orleans*, 580.
[2] Palfrey Plantation Diary, November 3, 12, 1862, May 25, 1863.
[3] Whittington (ed.), "Concerning the Loyalty of Slaves in Louisiana in 1863," *Louisiana Historical Quarterly*, XIV (October, 1931), 488.

Rouge as "an irrepressible rush of plantation negroes for their paradise of freedom."[1] A prominent St. Mary Parish cane producer recorded, "Negro man Joe... took the Yankee fever & absconded." Two days later, "Negress Mary Ann... took the same fever and absconded."[2] Another Bayou Teche planter in January of 1864 frequently entered in his journal, "Families of Negroes going into Yankee line."[3] Yankee fever remained virulent among the blacks throughout the war, and planters never could tell when the contagion would break out anew on their places.

The conduct of cane country Negroes toward whites was in general quite civil. Their pattern of departure from the plantations was simply that of slipping away during the night, and few instances of violence occurred, in view of the vast numbers of blacks in the region and the relative defenselessness of the whites. This complaisance was not universal, however, and outbreaks occasionally flared. Plantation folk lived in fear of servile insurrection during much of the war. Gangs of Negroes straying into New Orleans from places near the city frequently were riotous. An incident in August of 1862 was typical. A large group of unruly workers, complaining of overwork and short rations, armed themselves with cane knives, scythe blades, and clubs and marched upon the city. Police intercepted them in the outskirts of town, and in a pitched battle one Negro was killed and several wounded. The remainder were captured.[4]

At about the same time two policemen returning a Negro to a plantation below New Orleans were attacked by angry blacks. The Magnolia Plantation overseer gave his impression of the affair: "As they started to Return home Just after Leving Dunfords House They were fiered on from the cane field. Two of them woned and the other retreated to the city. The supposition is that they was fierd on by negroes which is no dout the fact."[5]

Federal commanders often felt deep sympathy for the Negroes and openly encouraged them to leave the plantations, or to resist discipline. General J. W. Phelps, commander of Camp Parapet at Carrollton, exemplified this school of thought. According to one of his officers, if

---

[1] New Orleans *Daily True Delta*, September 1, 1863.
[2] Palfrey Plantation Diary, November 6, 8, 1863.
[3] Bayside Plantation Journal, January 8, 1864.
[4] New Orleans *Daily True Delta*, August 5, 1862.
[5] Magnolia Plantation Journal, August 13, 1862.

General Phelps heard of a Negro being punished on a nearby plantation, he immediately dispatched troops to free the laborer. Even a worker convicted of barn-burning was liberated by his order. These acts, concluded the Northern observer, were most demoralizing to the blacks, "as they say they have only to go to the fort to be free." [1]

Encouraged by the attitude of officers like General Phelps, the Negroes sometimes became threatening, and on a few occasions violent. So ominous was the prospect of rebellion that General Weitzel, conqueror of the Bayou Lafourche territory, took alarm. He wrote on November 5, 1862, to General Butler warning of the symtoms of servile insurrection along the bayou. A terrible fear was among the inhabitants of Thibodaux, he said, where few able-bodied white men remained. "Women and children and even men, are in terror," he asserted. "It is heart-rending, and I cannot make myself responsible for it." He wrote again the same day, reiterating his fear of the laborers: "Relative to servile insurrection, I have the honor to inform you that on the plantation of Mr. David Pugh, a short distance from here, the Negroes who have returned... without provocation or cause of any kind refused this morning to work, and assaulted the overseer and Mr. Pugh, injuring them severely, also a gentleman who came to the assistance of Mr. Pugh. Upon the plantation also of Mr. W. J. Minor, on the Terre Bonne road, about sixteen miles from here, an outbreak has already occurred, and the entire community thereabout are in hourly expectation and terror of a general rising." [2]

On the Lafourche in the fall of 1862 occurred one of the rare cases of rape committed by plantation Negroes during the war. A Federal officer who served as recorder to the military court that tried and convicted the man wrote laconically, but with an implied touch of pathos, "A stolid plantation hand (with less intellect than a learned pig) who had criminally assaulted a white girl was condemned and hung." [3]

The advance of General Banks' army to the Red River in 1863 threw the Negroes of that area into the wildest excitement and stimulated occasional acts of violence against whites. The best eyewitness account of this furor was that of a planter who wrote to Governor Thomas O. Moore that the Negroes became "crazy." In their demoralization, all semblance of subordination and restraint was abandoned. Two of Gover-

---

[1] *The War of the Rebellion*, Ser. I, Vol. XV, 446.
[2] Butler, *Autobiography and Personal Reminiscences of Major-General Benjamin F. Butler*, 496-497.
[3] De Forest, *A Volunteer's Adventures*, 75.

nor Moore's Mooreland Plantation workers seized a Confederate soldier and forced him into the plantation stocks, after which they entertained themselves by abusing the helpless man. Drivers were, according to this planter, the worst offenders among the slaves.[1] Sudden Negro outbursts occurred in scattered parts of the sugar country for the duration of the conflict.

When from time to time the Confederate army pierced Federal lines and recovered territory previously lost, Negroes fled in panic before the Southerners. Their fears had foundation, for often returning Confederates dealt summary justice to those who had acted up when the Federals approached. Innocent Negroes also doubtless suffered. In the summer of 1863, as General Richard Taylor's army struck along the Lafourche, workers were terrified at his appearance. A Union officer described them as "in a state of exquisite alarm," and said that the entire black population of the Lafourche section made for the swamps in order to escape the wrath of counter-attacking Rebels.[2]

Negroes at Baton Rouge looked upon the Federal army's preparations for departure from that city with great apprehension, for "They feared the return of the rebels."[3] As the Northern columns withdrew from Alexandria in May of 1863, many Negroes accompanied the last wagon trains. The blacks were frightened because of mischief they had done when the Federals had approached, and their fears were sharpened by a report "that the 'rebel' soldiers were coming on down and killing negroes as they came...."[4] An episode on one of William J. Minor's plantations revealed the grim fate that the return of Southerners sometimes held for laborers. In May of 1863, while the Confederates had temporary possession of the region near Houma, they hanged one of Minor's Negroes, along with one belonging to a neighbor.[5] An indeterminable number of plantation workers died at the hands of avenging Southern campaigners.

The Negroes converted their abandonment of the plantations into a jubilee—an immense carousal of freedom. They flocked in gay mood to the levee as liberating Yankee steamboats paraded up the Mississippi,

---

[1] Whittington (ed.), "Concerning the Loyalty of Slaves in Louisiana in 1863," *Louisiana Historical Quarterly*, XIV (October, 1931), 492.
[2] De Forest, *Miss Ravenel's Conversion from Secession to Loyalty*, 272.
[3] Johns, *Life with the Forty-ninth Massachusetts Volunteers*, 162.
[4] Whittington (ed.), "Concerning the Loyalty of Slaves in Louisiana in 1863," *Louisiana Historical Quarterly*, XIV (October, 1931), 493.
[5] Minor Plantation Diary (1863), August 10.

and Federal soldiers aboard transports steaming for New Orleans were highly amused at sight of the black girls jauntily throwing kisses in their direction from the water's edge.[1]

Great camps of runaway Negroes sprang up at various places in the cane country. These shanty villages, packed with thousands of "freedom's children," were located near Union army posts, where the penniless wanderers depended upon Federal soldiers for food. Invading troops often looked to the fugitives for entertainment, and the result was a debauch of the blacks.[2] The availability and complaisance of slave women to Northern soldiers brought on a frolic of miscegenation. Effingham Lawrence of Magnolia Plantation was appalled at conditions prevalent among the thousands of laborers who congregated at Algiers across the river from New Orleans. He wrote with pity, "There [they] lived in the most abject misery Degredation & Filth." The blacks died by hundreds and were buried under the floors of salt warehouses in which they lived. To the great sugar proprietor, they presented "a scene Revolting to the sight and Repugnant to every sense of Humanity." His shocking summary was, "They were huddled together and Remained there Living in the most Loathsome manner and committing the most Dreadfull excesses of Depravity & Lechery in connexion with the soldiers of the camps—Presenting a spectacle of the most Revolting nature."[3]

Northern campaigners observed closely the behavior of the Negroes who followed the army, filling letters and diaries with accounts of their doings. Their manners and customs, wrote one Federal, gave an infinite variety of amusements to both officers and enlisted men. In camp at night the banjo and fiddle sounded, while the "Sable virgins of Africa could be seen 'tripping the light fantastic toe' with soldiers." Not infrequently these "sable nymphs" would be led into the darkness by a partner in uniform.[4] Union troops near Baton Rouge were captivated by the seductive dress of the Negro girls, which was described as low-necked, "half revealing dim charms" to ogling liberators.[5]

Planters shook their heads in disgust at the behavior of invading stalwarts with their laborers. "Soldiers & officers come on the place &

---

[1] Gould, *History of the First- Tenth- Twenty-ninth Maine Regiment*, 399.
[2] Kassel, *The Labor System of General Banks*, 41.
[3] Magnolia Plantation Journal, January 25, 1863.
[4] Smith, *Leaves from a Soldier's Diary*, 34.
[5] Johns, *Life with the Forty-ninth Massachusetts Volunteers*, 126.

go into the Quarters at all hours day & night....," an owner complained. "One soldier yesterday fastened his horse to a tree in the Quarter & remained in one of the houses for an hour."[1] These affairs between white men and Negro women should have come as no surprise to many of the planters.

Northerners sometimes were stunned to discover that their comrades visited the fleshpots while engaged in the noble crusade of emancipation. "I wish," sighed one disillusioned lad, "that it could be said that amalgamation is confined to the Southerners." He ruefully admitted that it was not. Meeting an old Negro woman on the levee, the soldier inquired of her how she supported herself since leaving the plantation. Her reply staggered him, for she said she was a midwife at camp. "Midwife at camp!" he gasped. "What on earth do soldiers in camp need midwives for?" "Oh!" she came back airily. "The darkey women fall in love with the Yankee soldiers, and I have to take care of the little mules."[2] Many such foals remained in the path of the Northern army.

Freed of restraint in matters of the spirit, the Negroes indulged without reserve in exhortations and prayer meetings. Laborers along the river above New Orleans lost themselves in preaching and singing from sundown on Saturdays until midnight on Sundays. Federal soldiers stood on the levee and listened to their plaintive songs. "The effect on the ears," thought one listener, "was like the effect of the great southern stream on our vision—powerful but not sweet."[3] Along the Lafourche in the fall of 1862 the Negroes engaged in various forms of religious expression. "Before one group," recalled an onlooker, "some old gray-headed patriarch would hold forth in a religious discourse, while another assembly of fugitives near by were enthralled in a prayer meeting."[4] Laborers on Bayou Teche flung themselves into a revel of gaiety in the day of liberation. Their camp glowed at night with the flames of a great bonfire, while fiddlers struck up spirited hoe-down tunes, and hundreds of dancers shuffled and whirled in the firelight. Suddenly cries of "Glory to God" and "Glory to Abe Linkum" rang out, and the dancing subsided into a prayer meeting, in which "Massa Linkum and the Linkum Sogers" were the names on every tongue.[5]

---

[1] Minor Plantation Diary (1863-1868), c. 1863.
[2] Johns, *Life with the Forty-ninth Massachusetts Volunteers*, 126.
[3] Calvert, *Reminiscences of a Boy in Blue*, 196.
[4] Smith, *Leaves from a Soldier's Diary*, 34.
[5] Van Alstyne, *Diary of an Enlisted Man*, 193-194.

The gravest problem facing planters who remained on their land after the invasion was that of procuring sufficient labor, for the great exodus that accompanied the advance of the Federal army practically stripped most plantations of workers. A New Orleans editor caught the true significance of the impact of invasion in a keen analysis of the sugar producers' plight, saying, "The difficulty of the Louisiana sugar planter will not be found in the imposition of a tax upon his product, but in depriving him of his labor. ..." Even as he wrote, many of the most valuable plantations in nearby parishes were rapidly falling into ruin because of the inducements and protection extended to slaves to come within the Northern camp lines. In September this writer pled with Federal authorities to put unemployed Negroes to work. Warning of the threat of levee crevasses and destructive overflows, he solemnly advised, "The swarms of idle, insolent and lazy negroes to be seen at Algiers and other camps, might be better employed. ..."[1]

Nor was the situation happy for Federal authorities in Louisiana, who found themselves embarrassed by thousands of vagrant Negroes appealing for rations and protection. General Butler was in a quandary. Should the United States army attempt to provide loaves and canned beef for these multitudes, or should the Negroes be forced back upon the plantations for sustenance? The emergency impelled him on November 28, 1862, to write to President Lincoln: "Many of the planters here, while professing loyalty, and I doubt not feeling it, if the 'institution' can be spared to them, have agreed together not to make any provision this autumn for another crop of sugar next season, hoping thereby to throw upon us this winter an immense number of blacks, without employment and without any means of support for the future. Thus—the government will be obliged to come to their terms for the future employment of the negroes, or to be at the enormous expenses to support them."[2]

The ingenious Butler ultimately hit upon an acceptable solution. He deemed it inadvisable to declare the blacks free, thereby saddling himself with their upkeep, but he could not in fact re-enslave them. The final decision was to hire as many as possible to planters who remained on their estates. Other Negroes were to be employed by government agents and lessees who operated abandoned plantations, while the army continued to provide for great numbers of them throughout the war.

---

[1] New Orleans *Daily True Delta*, July 27, September 28, 1862.
[2] Parton, *General Butler in New Orleans*, 527.

In the fall of 1862 General Butler took the first step to relieve the pressure of these throngs of idle Negroes, authorizing loyal planters in St. Bernard and Plaquemines Parishes to employ blacks at set wages—males to receive ten dollars a month, females and children lesser sums. The planters were to provide food, shelter, and medical care. The Negroes were to work ten hours a day, twenty-six days a month. General Butler prohibited corporal punishment, but allowed proprietors to report workers to local provost marshals for appropriate disciplinary action. The inception of the government policy of hiring vagrant Negroes and working abandoned and confiscated plantations came at the same time. On October 20 General Butler issued an order authorizing an agent named Charles A. Weed to take over a number of idle places on the river below New Orleans. Weed was to requisition labor from Negro camps, and supplies from the Quartermaster Department, and was to be paid a salary for his services. All receipts from the plantations were to go to the United States army.[1]

The experiment appeared to Union authorities to be a thrilling success, and in November General Butler expanded the plan of hiring Negroes throughout all of the plantation country that was in Federal hands. These measures, however, brought little relief to stricken planters. Negroes who had remained on the plantations after the arrival of the Northern army continued to work little and play much, and from time to time they grew surly and rebellious. Those on Woodland Plantation below New Orleans were in August of 1862 in a state of mutiny, according to an overseer, while a few days later the hands on nearby Oaklands Plantation refused to do a day's work, stating that they were half-fed and half-clothed, and that they had no intention of working any more than they already had.

During the fall conditions grew worse for proprietors as the Union army began to take possession of abandoned estates along the Mississippi. Effingham Lawrence opined that the Federals were agitating his laborers to drive him from his land in order that it might be seized. He declared, "We have a Terrible state of affairs, negroes Refusing to work and women all in their Houses." The blacks erected a gallows on his premises, saying that Union officers had told them to hang or drive away their master and overseer, and that they then would be free. The owner charged that the Northerners incited laborers on Pointe Celeste Plan-

---

[1] *Ibid.*, 523.

tation near Magnolia to drive the overseer from the place.[1]

Lawrence apparently had a firm grip on his workers, for he quieted them on November 1 with the promise of a "Handsome Present" if they would continue to work faithfully. They remained on the job, but the plantation's production dropped from more than 1,800 hogsheads in 1862 to 500 the next season. The owner was generally pleased with the conduct of his Negroes, considering the nature of affairs throughout the country, and he felt that his success in managing them was a vindication of slavery. "But there is one thing certain," he claimed. "On none of these places [where Negroes were paid wages] have the slaves done as well... as they have on Magnolia Plantation." The proud owner charged that attempts had been made on every side to lure his Negroes from the place, but that they had remained faithful and obedient, and were going ahead with a new crop. In spite of adverse circumstances brought on by enemy occupation, Lawrence was true to his promise of a present, and on January 24, 1863, he distributed $2,500 among the laborers as a bonus for their good conduct.[2]

General Butler quite naturally wished to report favorably on the outcome of his free labor plan, and on November 28, 1862, he wrote to President Lincoln, "Our experiment in attempting the cultivation of sugar by free labor, I am happy to report is succeeding admirably." He boasted that on one plantation a government agent had turned out more hogsheads of sugar in a day than ever had been accomplished on the same place by slave labor, and he concluded with a touch of smugness, "Your friend, Colonel Shaffer, has had put by, to be forwarded to you, a barrel of the finest sugar ever made by free black labor in Louisiana; and the fact that it will have no flavor of the degrading whip, will not, I know, render it less sweet to your taste."[3]

Butler did not remain in command of the Department of the Gulf long enough to test thoroughly his system. If he had, his conclusions might have been altered. Louisiana produced 87,000 hogsheads of sugar during the 1862-1863 season—a figure less than one fifth that of the previous year.[4] This was not an accurate index to the efficacy of free Negro labor, however, for reflected therein were all the wartime handicaps —destruction, abandonment, and general demoralization of the people.

---

[1] *Magnolia Plantation Journal*, August 16, October 21, 1862.
[2] *Ibid.*, January 25, 1863.
[3] Parton, *General Butler in New Orleans*, 525.
[4] *De Bow's Review*, IV, N. S. (September, 1867), 240.

A great factor, nevertheless, in the precipitate drop of sugar production was the lack of dependable labor.

General Butler turned over to General Banks in December of 1862 the thankless chore of providing for about 150,000 Negroes within the lines of the Department of the Gulf. Many of these workers were at the time employed in pursuance of Butler's order, on plantations within the Department. Some were on government establishments, but most of them were hired to "old planters," owners who had weathered invasion and remained on their land. General Banks wished to see the situation through the eyes of the Negroes, and he dispatched a commission of intelligent blacks to visit the plantations and investigate the needs of the workers. The sequestration commission was ordered to confer with planters and set up a labor system based upon its findings and those of the Negro investigating group.

A committee of prominent sugar growers called upon General Banks on January 12, 1863, in order to give him their views of the steps necessary to revive the flagging cane industry. The general met them with the sublime arrogance of an uninformed theorist, curtly declaring that he was not interested in their ideas on the management of Negroes, that they were full of "theories, & opinions based on the old system." "We must look to the new state of things," Banks announced smugly. "To the future and not to the past." He then turned prophet, saying that in three years the state would produce four times as much sugar as ever before.[1] Banks would live to see the supreme folly of these words; not for three decades would the Louisiana sugar output rival that of pre-war seasons.

General Banks moved ahead with his plans, instructing the sequestration commission to organize a labor system on a yearly contract basis similar to that already in existence. Planters were to provide workers with suitable wages, food, and clothing, while liens on the proprietors' crops covered their obligations. The commission was to pick up all idle blacks and place them on abandoned lands, where the army would employ them. The commission implemented these instructions with an order authorizing owners and laborers to draw up contracts for the following year. Negroes were pledged to "work faithfully and industriously, and maintain a respectful and subordinate deportment toward their employers," and planters were told to respect scrupulously the terms of the contracts.

---

[1] Minor Plantation Diary (1863), January 8.

The new wage scale provided that mechanics, sugar makers, and drivers receive three dollars a month, male field hands two dollars, and female field hands, house servants, and nurses one dollar. In addition to these wages, sugar producers were to furnish food, lodging, and medical care for the workers, and support for their dependents. If the cane growers and laborers agreed, one twentieth of the profit from the year's crop could be paid to the hands in lieu of monthly wages.[1] Two great differences between this system and slavery were that the Negroes now could contract to work for planters of their choice, and discipline was administered by Federal provost marshals rather than by owners.

Planters went about during the winter and spring of 1863 making contracts with as many Negroes as they could round up. William J. Minor drew up an agreement by the terms of which his laborers would receive one twentieth of the crop. His plan was to mark one hogshead out of every twenty with the letters "N.S." When the sugar was sold, money from these hogsheads was to be distributed to the workers on a share basis. Mechanics were to get three shares each, field hands two each, and women, nurses, and "half hands"—boys and girls—one each. Minor took steps to maintain discipline among laborers, ruling that no Negro should leave the place without a pass. But he cautioned his overseer that the lash should not be used "at present" in enforcing the order, for he feared that the laborers would desert him at slightest provocation. In April of 1863 he instructed his overseer to permit them to haul moss to Houma. The overseer was to refrain from using harsh language and to obey meticulously all orders of the local provost marshal. Negroes were permitted religious services, "So long as the religious ones behave[d] well."[2]

Cane country blacks worked desultorily during the spring and summer of 1863. In the absence of the old type of discipline, they were prone to trifle. A planter stated in March that laborers on his Terrebonne Parish estate were acting "villainously," and that he had hopes only of making enough seed cane for the next season.[3]

Grinding season of 1863 brought increased pressure upon plantation workers and again put to test the Federal scheme of free labor. In October

---

[1] Banks, *Emancipated Labor in Louisiana*, 33.
[2] Minor Plantation Diary (1861-1868), February 12, 1863. Spanish moss, which abounds in lower Louisiana, was used for stuffing cushions and mattresses.
[3] Sitterson, "The McCollams; a Planter Family of the Old and New South," *Journal of Southern History*, VI (August, 1940), 359-360.

a letter to the editor of the New Orleans *Bee* predicted a meager crop in Plaquemines Parish as the result of a scarcity of labor.[1] Along Bayou Lafourche workers were hard to find, and once found they were often lazy and inefficient.[2] A New Orleans journalist warned on October 19 that from 10,000 to 15,000 hogsheads of sugar were in danger of being lost from lack of labor, and he reiterated an old plea that Federal authorities force thousands of idle blacks in the city to work in the harvest.[3]

William J. Minor painted a black picture of free Negro labor, lamenting that workers stole everything they could lay hands on, and that they spent most of their time hauling moss to Houma in plantation carts. To the planter's indignation, they cut down the finest trees on the place in order to get the moss. He concluded pessimistically that overseers had lost all control over the Negroes, with the result that these employees were useless.[4] The next month Minor learned that his laborers were hiring out, for their own profit, his carts and teams to the townspeople of Houma, upon which he commented glumly: "Oliver had a hand in this... Yet he is one of the religious ones—Their religion does not prevent them from Stealing, lying & other vices." The final straw came when workers dawdled in the harvest. The planter recorded in November that they refused to go into the field before breakfast, allowed kettles to boil out of juice, and fed rollers too slowly. Throughout the fall the blacks malingered, refusing to get up in the morning because the weather was too cold, and leaving the sugarhouse in order to gather their own corn. The sick rate was incredible. Suddenly, in the middle of the afternoon a Negro would walk out of the cane field; all of the others would follow, and work was ended for the day. The Negroes sometimes refused to work at night, which meant that fires would go out under the boilers, thus causing an immense waste in time and fuel, and endangering the crop to ruinous frost. "The wish of the negro is now the white man's law," brooded Minor. "A man had as well be in pergatory as attempt to work a sugar plantation, under existing circumstances."

Negro women were the worst offenders. With exaggerated independence they refused to put in a full day of work. "The sucklers," said Minor, "are the most lazy insolent and worthless." He declared that they usually got to the field at about nine-thirty in the morning, worked

---

[1] New Orleans *Bee*, October 14, 1863.
[2] New Orleans *Daily True Delta*, October 15, 1863.
[3] New Orleans *Bee*, October 19, 1863.
[4] Minor Plantation Diary (1863), September 5.

until eleven-thirty, returned to work at three in the afternoon, and quit at five. One black woman, Kitty Johnson, led this Civil War sit-down movement, retorting insolently if told that she did not work enough to support herself.[1]

Minor's emotions toward his laborers appeared in an interesting list of names in the back of his diary. Under the provocative heading, "Faithful among the Faithless—Faithful only they," the proprietor wrote the names of twenty-eight Negroes. From time to time the faithful wavered, and beside many names the owner jotted, "Fell from grace." In front of numerous names were the words, "Fight," "Threats," and "Knife." The truculent Kitty Johnson's name drew the distinctive comment, "The insolence & lies of this woman exceed belief." Names of five Negro families were placed in a separate column under the caption, "Worthless or Insolent & not worth Keeping." Some of the blacks, on the other hand, remained faithful. By the name of one worker, Kitty Perkins, Minor paid this tribute, "Has worked all the morning in a cold rain putting up hay." Beside the names of several Negroes he listed produce given them as bonuses for diligent service, and he occasionally penned such notes as, "Peter Williams & Hany Taylor must be remembered."[2]

On January 1, 1863, President Lincoln issued his emancipation proclamation setting free the slaves of owners in areas still in rebellion. Lincoln exempted from this action various parts of the South already under Federal control, including thirteen of the lower sugar parishes.[3] The reaction of masters in the upper parishes was interesting. An observer in the vicinity of Baton Rouge—a portion of the sugar land still considered in rebellion—declared that owners made no attempt to conceal the proclamation from their slaves. One producer called his hands together and read the document to them, explaining the meaning of its terms, and stating that the Negroes need not rebel in order to get their freedom. "[You] need not endanger [your] own lives or stain [your] hands with blood-shed," he said, "for [you] are now at liberty to go if [you] please." The Negroes realized that merely walking off the plantation would not benefit them in any way and replied that they had no desire to leave.

---

[1] Minor Plantation Diary (1863-1868), September 29, October 12, November 11, 14, 16, 27, 1863.

[2] *Ibid.*, list of workers in back of diary.

[3] John Rose Ficklen, *History of Reconstruction in Louisiana through 1868* (Baltimore, 1910), 124.

When asked why they did not take this opportunity to go free, an intelligent slave replied: "I see no use of us going and getting ourselves into trouble. If so be it we are to get free, we get it anyhow.... We think it betterer to stay home on the plantation, and get our food and our clothes. If we are to get freedom, dare we are! But, if we run away, and go to New Orleans, like dem crazy niggers, where is we?"[1] This Negro possessed the insight to remain docile and continue being provided with the necessities of life while the whites decimated themselves in a contest to decide his future.

Another sugar cultivator read the proclamation to his slaves and interpreted it in such a manner as to ridicule it in their eyes. He pointed out that the decree applied only to areas not in Federal hands; that Negroes in sections held by the Union army were still slaves. The crafty master then explained: "This place [West Baton Rouge Parish] is uncertain. Both parties claim it, and we don't know which Government it is under. If it is under Lincoln's Government, then he says in that proclamation that you are to be slaves; but if it is under Jefferson Davis's Government, then he (Lincoln) says in that proclamation that you are to be free. So I can't tell you what you are to be until we see which government we are going to be under. But there is one thing that I can tell you, that is, if you are within Jefferson Davis's country Mr. Lincoln says you are to be free, though I doubt it very much, because he has not the power there to make you free. But if you are in New Orleans or any place within the lines held by Mr. Lincoln's armies, then Mr. Lincoln says you are to be slaves, and there is no doubt about that, because he has there the power to make and keep you slaves."[2]

The conscription of Negro men into the Federal army further diminished the precarious labor supply. The activity of a Northern soldier in the summer of 1863 in making a list of the names of planters and the number of Negroes on each place aroused suspicion among landowners, one of whom surmised, "This I presume is preparatory to a draft of the negro men."[3] The Union authorities on August 17, 1863, took ten men from William J. Minor's Hollywood and Southdown Plantations, and from time to time throughout the summer and fall additional blacks were taken. These seizures often were accompanied by "deep distress" among the families of the men, and when a distraught Negro requested Minor

---

[1] Watson, *Life in the Confederate Army*, 429-430.
[2] *Ibid.*, 430.
[3] Minor Plantation Diary (1863), August 17.

to take care of his family, the planter stated, "I will do all I can for them."[1]

Federal seizure of Negroes was sometimes high-handed and without warning. In November of 1863 a squad of soldiers rushed suddenly into a field on Bayou Cypre Mort where laborers were gathering corn. Thirteen Negro men were hustled away without the opportunity of taking leave of their families, and two days later another Union detachment returned and took away in the same manner three additional workers.[2] The conscription of plantation Negroes continued to harrass sugar producers throughout the war. A Union soldier stationed in St. Mary Parish in the summer of 1864 pictured the reaction of the blacks to Federal impressment, saying that when conscripting officers came up from New Orleans "... the colored women appeared nearly frantic when they were parted from their men."[3]

The handicaps of inefficient labor, interference by military authorities, and the activities of Union conscription officers hampered but did not stop planters from making a crop. Producers struggled to maintain plantation routine, and sugar making with hired Negro labor proceeded during the fall and winter of 1863. Northerners on junket to sugar establishments discovered a variety of opinions among proprietors regarding the value of free labor. Most agents and lessees of government plantations looked with far greater approval upon the experiment than did "old planters." On December 3 a Federal investigating commission visited plantations along the river below New Orleans, observing conditions on Pointe Celeste, Sarah, Oaklands, and Star Plantations. Pointe Celeste and Sarah were in the hands of government agents; Oaklands and Star were leased from Union authorities by a loyal woman. All of these places had been abandoned by their owners and taken over by the Federal army. The commission found what it sought, and the free labor system was declared an overwhelming success.

A few days later a large group of observers, including Military Governor G. F. Shepley and Mrs. Nathaniel P. Banks, journeyed down the river to Magnolia and Woodland Plantations to witness the progress of free labor, but they were disappointed in their findings. The manager of the two estates reported that he supplemented the Negro labor force with whites, who could do four times as much work per man. A party of

---

[1] Minor Plantation Diary (1863-1868), August 17, September 19, 1863.
[2] Palfrey Plantation Diary, November 9, 11, 1863.
[3] Marshall, *Army Life; from a Soldier's Journal*, 398.

New Yorkers and Bostonians journeyed on December 25 to the Rost plantation near New Orleans. This establishment was operated by a Northern firm that leased from the government numerous abandoned places. The visitors inspected the sugarhouse and watched the process of sugar making, then went to the dwelling house where they enjoyed a fine dinner and were entertained by Negro singers and dancers. Sumptuously wined and dined, these sight-seers, who probably knew nothing about sugar making, pompously called free Negro labor a great success. [1]

By the end of 1863 the deteriorating sugar industry exposed the error of General Banks' hasty and ill-advised promise of a year earlier, at which time he had rashly predicted a sensational recovery of sugar as the result of free labor. The picture instead was more discouraging than ever. Total sugar production of the 1863-1864 season was 76,801 hogsheads. The yield had dropped more than 10,000 hogsheads since the previous season and would have been much smaller, had not much of the crop been grown from stubble cane. [2]

The problem of dealing with vagrant Negroes and abandoned and confiscated plantations continued throughout the war to vex commanders of the Department of the Gulf. Late in 1863 James E. Yeatman, President of the Western Sanitary Commission, investigated conditions of Negroes in the lower Mississippi Valley and submitted a report in which he outlined in detail a plan for free Negro labor. Many of his suggestions were similar to measures already in effect under General Banks, but in addition to a wage scale for blacks, Yeatman called for abandoned plantations to be leased to Negroes by the government. He also recommended that a number of places be set aside as colonies, under government agents, for destitute Negroes. [3] These colonies were comparable to the displaced persons' camps of modern war. On July 2, 1864, Congress passed an act placing the Treasury Department in charge of Negro affairs and abandoned lands. The Secretary of the Treasury appointed W. P. Mellen supervising agent in the lower Mississippi Valley, with Yeatman as assistant agent. [4]

In the meantime General Banks was confronted with the actual emergency of caring for thousands of idle and often lazy Negroes, while

---

[1] New Orleans *Era*, December 3, 25, 1863.
[2] *De Bow's Review*, IV, N. S. (September, 1867), 240.
[3] James E. Yeatman, *Suggestions of a Plan of Organization for Freed Labor* (St. Louis, 1864), 3.
[4] Paul S. Peirce, *The Freedmen's Bureau* (Iowa City, 1904), 23-24.

plantations continued to deteriorate for want of labor. On February 3, 1864, Banks attempted to deal with the problem by issuing new regulations covering Negro affairs. His order duplicated most of the provisions of the sequestration commission's instructions of a year earlier. Planters were to grade laborers into four classes according to merit. Wages ranged from three dollars a month for the lowest class to eight dollars for the highest. The penalty for crime or indolence was forfeiture of pay, and proprietors might also dock wages in case of sickness. Provost marshals remained judges in disciplinary cases. Planters were to provide workers with cabins, food, clothes, medical care, and a garden plot for each family.[1]

During the summer of 1864 General Banks created a bureau of free labor, with Chaplain Thomas W. Conway in charge. The establishment of this organization resulted in a confusing overlap of authority in Negro affairs in the cane country, for both Chaplain Conway and Treasury Department Agent Mellen claimed jurisdiction.[2]

While the armies contended for supremacy, and cane planters strove to harvest crops, events on all fronts moved inexorably toward emancipation of the slaves. General Butler at Fort Monroe, Virginia, before the invasion of Louisiana had refused to return "contrabands" to their owners—an initial step in the liberation process. Though the premature freeing of slaves by General John C. Frémont in Missouri in 1861 and by General David Hunter in parts of Georgia, Florida, and South Carolina in 1862 was repudiated by the Lincoln government, these moves were part of the trend toward freedom. On July 17, 1862, Congress seized the initiative, enacting that slaves of masters supporting the rebellion and United States soldier-slaves were free. Lack of coordination between Congress and the President, however, made these acts ineffective.

The orders of General Butler and General Banks relative to Negro labor in Louisiana waived the legal question of emancipation, taking for granted the obvious *de facto* freedom of all blacks under Union authority. President Lincoln's emancipation proclamation of January 1, 1863, freed no slaves in loyal Louisiana—that is, occupied Louisiana—and Lincoln had no power actually to set free anyone in Confederate Louisiana. The situation at the end of 1863 was that the Negroes of that portion of the state within Federal lines were in fact free and were receiving wages for labor, though no authority had manumitted them,

---
[1] *The War of the Rebellion*, Ser. I, Vol. XXXIV, Pt. II, 227-231.
[2] Peirce, *The Freedmen's Bureau*, 18.

while those within the Confederate sphere were in fact slaves, though the President of the United States had declared them free.[1] General Banks proclaimed inoperative in January of 1864 all laws in Louisiana recognizing and regulating slavery. This presumably set free from a legal point of view all Negroes in Union Louisiana, though the courts were confused as to the efficacy of the action. This confusion was ended when in September the Louisiana constitutional convention declared all slaves in the state free.[2]

Proprietors began in the winter of 1864 to contract with Negroes for the coming year under the terms of General Banks' recent order. In issuing instructions concerning laborers, one planter stated emphatically that the Negroes must be required to work nine hours a day in winter months and ten hours a day during other months of the year. All lost time, no matter from what cause, was to be deducted in paying the workers. Overseers were to take care that the hands were credited only with the exact amount of time that they actually worked. "If the forfeiture of wages does not make them work," instructed the planter, "their rations of all Kinds must be Stoped & if that does not make them work they must be put off the place."[3] Free Negro labor remained unpredictable and often unsatisfactory. In March a landowner wrote that the blacks on Bayou Teche were "insolent and refractory."[4] A planter who had trouble keeping his laborers on the job put into effect in May a policy of deducting from one quarter of a day's to a week's wages for disobedience of an order.[5]

Plantation affairs grew so chaotic during the fall of 1864 that General Banks was forced to admit defeat. This officer, who two years earlier had lectured the cane growers on the virtues of free labor and had predicted a fourfold increase in sugar output within three years, tacitly conceded the failure of his system by inviting the very planters whom he previously had rebuffed to write letters of advice on the resuscitation of sugar culture. This overture brought a flurry of replies condemning free labor in positive and sometimes flaming language.

On October 13 "A Planter" delivered the opening salvo against the new system. With blistering sarcasm he reminded Banks of his wild

---

[1] Wiley, *Southern Negroes, 1861-1865*, 211-216, *passim*.
[2] *Ibid.*, 217.
[3] Minor Plantation Diary (1861-1865), February 22, 1864.
[4] Palfrey Plantation Diary, March 16, 1864.
[5] Minor Plantation Diary (1861-1865), May 23, 1864.

prophecy, pointing out that two years had elapsed, and instead of an increase in production, many planters had no corn, and in some parishes there was not enough seed cane to plant one fourth of the land formerly in cultivation. The irate proprietor claimed that his male workers wasted during the previous grinding season one sixth of the working time, and that the females dawdled away one third of the time. He scoffed at the idea of starving the laborers into working, saying that it was cheaper to feed them from the storeroom than to drive them into stealing livestock. With a vicious cut at government plantations, he declared that if it were possible to starve Negroes, they would have died on those places run by Federal agents. "Some call this [government plantation] the model farm," the writer sneered. "But I know not for what reason, unless it be that its occupants live without work." The scornful planter claimed that he could not get laborers to repair fences, buildings, or ditches. They insisted on doing nothing but working in cane. Sanitary conditions in the cabins were deplorable. "High wages," he concluded, "will not make a lazy negro, industrious." [1]

A few days later another sugar grower launched a condemnation of the free labor plan. The year 1863 was a good season for cane, he said, except for poor labor. His plantation should have produced 800 hogsheads of sugar. Instead, by hiring forty white workers, in addition to Negroes, and by purchasing $2,000 worth of wood, which should have been cut on the place, the owner managed to put up 400 hogsheads, and he expected to make only about 50 hogsheads during the 1864-1865 season. "Stealing is the order of the day," was the cultivator's parting shot. [2] An "Old Planter" joined the hue and cry, attacking the pilfering and thieving of the blacks. In twelve months his laborers had stolen more than $1,000 worth of copper from his sugarhouse, sending it out in bales of moss. Harrows, hoes, plows, axes, and saws disappeared, he charged, and so many hogs, sheep, and poultry were stolen that he was forced to buy this produce from the blacks. "Demoralization of the sexes is shocking," he continued. "They work less, have less respect, are less orderly than ever." [3] The most prominent planters of Terrebonne Parish met in November to discuss sugar possibilities for the coming year and agreed that free Negro labor had proved a complete failure. [4]

---

[1] New Orleans *Times*, October 13, 1864.
[2] *Ibid.*, October 21, 1864.
[3] *Ibid.*, November 2, 1864.
[4] Minor Plantation Diary (1863-1868), November 17, 1864.

In the fall of 1864 Benjamin F. Flanders replaced W. P. Mellen as supervising special agent of Negro affairs for the Treasury Department. Flanders announced on October 26 that he was ready to take charge of all freedmen in the department.[1] For a few months landowners were subject to Flanders' regulations, but in March of the next year General Stephen A. Hurlbut, successor to General Banks, issued an order superseding all previous instructions and bringing Negro affairs back under the army.[2] Congress on March 3 passed an act establishing in the War Department a Bureau of Refugees, Freedmen, and Abandoned Lands, and this new agency—commonly known as the Freedmen's Bureau—soon took over the management of Negro labor in the cane country.[3]

While administrative changes occurred, and confusion became worse confounded, the sugar industry continued to dissolve. Flanders assembled the leading planters of lower Louisiana in November of 1864 for a conference, and once again the cane growers were able to discuss their grievances. They told Flanders that the Negroes were lazy, dishonest, and insolent; that they would work only in the presence of the provost marshals. As soon as these officers turned their backs, the laborers lapsed into old habits of slothfulness. Efforts to punish them by withholding rations were a farce, as the blacks were masters of the art of foraging. The cane growers desired laws making workers responsible for teams and equipment. The blacks should be prohibited from owning any livestock, felt the cultivators, because this created a tendency to steal corn. Negroes should be required to have passes in order to leave the plantations, and a nine o'clock curfew would have a salutary effect. The cane growers essentially asked for a return to a situation as near to slavery as possible. Flanders refused to set up this form of discipline, which obviously would have been odious to the workers, and the meeting brought no effective action for the rebuilding of the stricken economy.[4]

Flanders published new instructions in February of 1865 regarding the hiring of Negroes. Wages were set at twenty-five, twenty, and fifteen dollars a month for the various classes of male workers and at eighteen, fourteen, and ten dollars for female laborers. Negroes were to purchase their own food and clothing, while proprietors were to furnish cabins

---

[1] *The War of the Rebellion*, Ser. I, Vol. XLVIII, Pt. I, 492-493.
[2] *Ibid.*, 1146-1148. General Hurlbut replaced General Banks as commander of the Department of the Gulf on September 23, 1864.
[3] Peirce, *The Freedmen's Bureau*, 129.
[4] New Orleans *Times*, November 22, 1864.

and other necessities. Local Treasury Department agents replaced provost marshals in maintaining discipline, and deductions and forfeitures of wages were to be made only by approval of these officials.[1] Scarcely was the ink dry on the regulations when General Hurlbut declared them null and void and brought the hiring of laborers back under his supervision. The terms of his order were similar to those of General Banks' instructions of the previous year, except that wages were different. Male workers were to receive from six to ten dollars a month, women from five to eight dollars. Boys under fourteen years of age were to be paid three dollars a month, and girls two dollars. Landowners were to provide cabins, food, clothing, medical care, and garden plots in which the Negroes could grow their own vegetables. Hurlbut made one concession to the landowners, for he forbade workers to own livestock.[2]

The sugar crop of 1864-1865 dropped to approximately 10,000 hogsheads,[3] a debacle for which the inefficiencies of free Negro labor in its trial stage were largely responsible. The "insolence, indolence, and demoralization" of the freedmen—to borrow planters' terms—were natural outgrowths of the times. For a people fresh out of bondage to spend a season in the wilderness of irresponsibility and unrest was not without precedent, even in the Old Testament. Nor could the unschooled and inexperienced blacks know that freedom meant freedom to work, not freedom from work. Added to the exuberance that naturally flowed from liberation was a strong desire among the Negroes to possess their own land, an ambition stirred by the promises of crusading Northern soldiers and others of less exalted motive. Disappointment at finding themselves herded back upon the very plantations from which they recently had been freed—a process in which Federal authorities and landowners were allied—doubtless contributed to the acrimony of the laborers.

Most Louisiana sugar growers firmly believed that without slave labor their plantations would be worthless. Bred in this conviction, they permitted *a priori* condemnation to blind them to the possibility of any good in the new order, just as Federal authorities were led by their preconceptions vastly to exaggerate its immediate virtues. Bitterness

---

[1] *Ibid.*, February 5, 1865.
[2] *The War of the Rebellion*, Ser. I, Vol. XLVIII, Pt. I, 1146-1148.
[3] *De Bow's Review*, IV, N.S. (September, 1867), 240.

over defeat and military occupation robbed cultivators of the insight to perceive that Union officials in large measure shared their own views of the role of the Negro, which were that at least for the present he should remain a laborer and not become a landowner. In the meantime, under the combination of planter prejudice, Negro unpredictability, and official intransigence the output of sugar plummeted to less than three per cent of the pre-war yield, and the plantation economy fell apart.

CHAPTER IX

FROM EXULTATION TO DESPAIR

War stunned the cane planters, who saw their homes overrun and often ruined, and their sons ride away to battle, many never to return. Sugar proprietors often were torn from their families, and a lack of communications made these separations far more galling than they would have been under normal circumstances. The exigencies of defeat called for a re-examination of political allegiance and brought a shifting of attitude toward the military situation. These varying emotions of the planters under the impact of invasion and military occupation threw into high relief the strengths and weaknesses of their character.

The mind of the cane country oscillated violently between despondency and elation during the great ordeal. In the spring of 1862 planters were steeped in gloom at the knowledge that New Orleans was in enemy hands and that a great battle recently had raged around the obscure little Shiloh Church on the bank of the distant Tennessee River. The fear lingered that thousands of Southern boys, including hundreds from families in the bayou land, probably lay dead or wounded, and one sugar producer thoughtfully purchased large quantities of jelly to be sent to Corinth, Mississippi, for the recently defeated Confederates.[1]

Southern success, on the other hand, fired the hearts of lower Louisiana planters. They reveled in a report in May of 1862 that a superior force of Federals had been routed near Richmond, Virginia. According to the account that reached the sugar land, Generals Joseph E. Johnston and Robert E. Lee had both been killed in battle, but President Jefferson Davis had personally led the troops to triumph. "Too good to be true," one cane producer exulted.[2] General Richard Taylor's counterattack along the Lafourche in the summer of 1862 brought unbridled joy to many cane country inhabitants. "Another glorious victory yesterday," penned a jubilant Bayou Teche landowner. "It is supposed [the Confederates] will now march on N. Orleans."[3]

Planters sought war news avidly and speculated freely on the military

---

[1] Minor Plantation Diary (1861-1862), May 1, 1862.
[2] *Ibid.*, May 4, 1862.
[3] Palfrey Plantation Diary, June 25, 1863.

situation. In the fall of 1862 word spread that Donaldsonville had been destroyed by the Union navy. Landowners were aware that this fate had come upon the town because of the injudicious firing by guerillas upon enemy gunboats. "These attacks should not have been made till we were ready to repell an attack from the enemy," a proprietor sagaciously remarked. "I expect to be ruined by the stupidity of others before this war is over."[1]

Rumors flooded the countryside. A girl's jottings illustrated the extravagance of many of these reports: "News comes pouring in. Note we a few items, to see how many will prove false. First, we have taken Baltimore without firing a gun; Maryland has risen en masse to join our troops; Longstreet and Lee are marching on Washington from the rear; the Louisiana troops are ordered home to defend their own state—thank God! if it will only bring the boys back!"[2] Cane growers were aware of Lee's invasion of Pennsylvania and awaited breathlessly the outcome of the great Confederate stroke. Word circulated that Vicksburg and Port Hudson had surrendered to the Federals, and a landowner sagely warned that the fall of these Mississippi River strongholds and the repulse of Lee at Gettysburg marked the beginning of the end for the South. New Orleans buzzed with reports that France and Spain were to intervene in the war, but a wary planter suspected that brokers and moneylenders had filled the town with these predictions in order to keep it in a state of excitement and promote their own interests. "They should be hung," he snarled.[3]

Northern military success in the cane parishes made it possible for the Unionist element among sugar growers to come to the front in plantation affairs. The size of this group is indeterminable, for by 1865 less than 200 sugar plantations out of 1,291 were still in operation. Proprietors of all of these active establishments were nominal Unionists, for they could not have cultivated their land without taking the oath of allegiance to the United States. But many of them were pseudo-Unionists, who at heart remained loyal to the Southern cause and out of what might be called an enlightened self-interest collaborated with the invaders, explaining their change of face with the oft-quoted statement, "Self-preservation is the first law of nature."[4]

---

[1] Minor Plantation Diary (1861-1862), November 1, 1862.
[2] Dawson, *A Confederate Girl's Diary*, 226.
[3] Minor Plantation Diary (1863), July 6, 12.
[4] Watson, *Life in the Confederate Army*, 424.

The case of William J. Minor exemplified the full emotional cycle of a Unionist cane planter. Throughout the 1850's Minor staunchly opposed secession. As the Confederacy was forming he took an interest in Southern political affairs, but probably was more concerned with gaining tariff concessions for sugar cultivators than with secession. By 1862 he had caught the fever of the gray cause. His sons were in the Confederate army, and he exulted in news of Southern victories in Virginia and sent food to Confederate troops in Tennessee. Shocked by the surrender of New Orleans and the decline of the Confederate military situation in the West, Minor reverted to Unionism, which doubtless had remained imbedded in his conscience all of the time. By 1863 he looked upon secession as a stupendous act of folly. "I foresaw (or thought I did) the terrible woes that would result from it & opposed it most strenuously," he truthfully lamented. "Would have prevented it by force if I had the power." He anathematized the military leaders: "What kind of hearts must those men have who are carrying on this war for *Selfish* purposes. Is there any punishment here or hereafter adiquate to their deserts— I fear not."[1]

Sugar growers who remained in operation after the Federal invasion formed the conservative wing of a Unionist group that attempted to restore Louisiana to the Union during the war. They desired two things in the new state government—retention of slavery and maintenance of the Louisiana constitution of 1852. This constitution based legislative representation upon total population, thereby giving a preponderance of political power to the black belt parishes dominated by the great slave owners. The most determined effort of the planters to gain their political ends came in November of 1863, at which time they held an unauthorized election of state and Federal officials. This attempt to restore Louisiana to the Union and at the same time revert to the social and political status of the pre-war period came to naught. Congress denied seats to the members elected, and the state constitutional convention of 1864 provided for the emancipation of slaves in Louisiana and based legislative representation upon the number of qualified voters, which at the time meant white men.[2]

Many plantation folk steadfastly retained their theories regarding the righteousness and necessity of Negro slavery. A Louisiana girl exclaimed:

---

[1] Minor Plantation Diary (1863-1868), December 20, 1863, January 2, 1864.
[2] Caskey, *Secession and Restoration of Louisiana*, 86.

"And to think Old Abe wants to deprive us of all that fun! No more cotton, sugar-cane, or rice! No more old black aunties or uncles! No more rides in mule teams, no more songs in the cane-field, no more steaming kettles, no more black faces and shining teeth around the furnace fires." She described a sugarhouse scene where Negroes were gay, though deferential, and scoffed that perhaps some "good old Abolitionist" was needed to tell the slaves how miserable they were.[1] Most of the citizens of the cane parishes did not dream of the possibility of making sugar without Negro slavery.

Relations between invading soldiers and plantation folk usually were less galling to Louisiana citizens than was to be expected under such trying circumstances. Physical violence against civilians was rare. An observer wrote that plantation owners were humbly thankful for guards put on their premises to drive away Negroes, deserters, and jayhawkers.[2] Northern soldiers almost without exception kept their distance from plantation women. A mistress demonstrated this respect for her sex with a story about a Northern guard—a young German-American— once assigned to her place. As this youth entered the yard he plucked a rose. "See," cried one of the plantation girls indignantly. "That mean Yankee is taking our flowers!" "It is a good sign," replied the older woman, "that he will never do us any greater harm." She was right, for when the young sentry left, he was a friend of the entire household.[3] When a Union detachment appeared at a plantation near Baton Rouge in the summer of 1862 the raiders refrained from entering the house upon being informed that the mistress was pregnant. Their decorum was such that one of the household slaves opined, "I don't believe them men would 'onderscend' to steal spoons."[4]

Not all contacts were this pleasant. On General Butler was focused the most intense hatred and loathing. A letter from a plantation woman, written a few days after the fall of New Orleans, gave insight into the spirit of the times: "But Yankee, proud Yankee! drest in a little brief authority, when our gallant Beauregard comes to deliver us from the inflated myrmidon of the tyrannical Buffon at Washington, we shall see with intense joy the noble Picayune Butler flying from the Vatican, in finished Bull Run or Bethel style, with all the Yankee rabble infesting

---

[1] Dawson, *A Confederate Girl's Diary*, 278.
[2] De Forest, *A Volunteer's Adventures*, 76.
[3] Merrick, *Old Times in Dixie Land*, 36.
[4] Ripley, *From Flag to Flag*, 23.

our city at his heels." [1] Effingham Lawrence wrote in towering fury of a raid by Northern soldiers in the summer of 1862 on a plantation below New Orleans. The planter said that troops commanded by General Neal Dow pillaged the estate, took the owner prisoner, and broke into his daughters' bedrooms in the middle of the night. "The conduct towards his daughters who were in Bed when the officers and negroes Broke into the Rooms," stormed the proprietor, "was an act upon a peaceable Family unparalleled in the history of the world." [2]

Other episodes revealed the searing passions that rose out of the war in the bayou land. A formation of Union troops was fired on near the town of Houma, with two men killed and two wounded. Citizens of the community refused aid to the wounded and inflicted terrible indignities on the dead, stamping their faces with boot heels. Colonel John A. Keith of the Northern army, understandably outraged, seized hostages and uttered threats of executions in retaliation. [3] In the spring of 1863 a planter's son was arrested by the Federals on the charge of cutting telegraph lines in Terrebonne Parish. The father was told that the captain of the steamboat which took the captive to New Orleans chained him on the upper deck, where he would be exposed to guerilla fire from the banks of the river. [4] Northern soldiers took small arms from the landowners in spite of vehement protests that the weapons were badly needed for protection against stragglers and marauders. [5]

The more bitter of the plantation folk never lost an opportunity to vent wrath on the invaders. Girls near New Iberia in 1863 taunted Federal prisoners who were being escorted to camps in Texas. According to one of the captives, two pretty "young ladies" stopped their carriage and "greatly refreshed" the marchers by telling them that they hoped they would be hanged at the end of the lane, as such a fate was well-deserved by "nigger-thieves." [6]

A Northern campaigner at Port Hudson found nothing refreshing about the venom of plantation women, whose fury he later described in powerful fiction: "[They were] full of scorn and hatred; so unwomanly,

---

[1] Jessie A. Marshall (ed.), *Private and Official Correspondence of General Benjamin F. Butler during the Period of the Civil War*, 5 vols. (Norwood, Massachusetts, 1917), I, 448.
[2] Magnolia Plantation Journal, August 9, 1862.
[3] Minor Plantation Diary (1861-1862), May 28, 1862.
[4] Minor Plantation Diary (1863), March 24.
[5] Palfrey Plantation Diary, September 23, 1863.
[6] Charles C. Nott, *Sketches of the War* (New York, 1865), 66.

so unimaginably savage in conversation and soul that no novelist would dare to invent such characters; nothing but real life could justify him in painting them. They seemed to be intoxicated with the strength of a malice, passionate enough to dethrone the reason of any being not aboriginally brutal. They laughed to see the wounds and hear the groans of the sufferers. They jeered them because the assault had failed. The Yankees never could take Port Hudson; they were the meanest, the most dastardly people on earth. Joe Johnston would soon kill the rest of them, and have Banks a prisoner, and shut him up in a cage." [1] This picture is doubtless overdrawn, but the rage of these women, who witnessed the wrecking of their homes, and whose husbands and brothers were possibly fighting in the Confederate army trapped in Port Hudson, can easily be imagined. If Louisiana troops had been storming a town in this soldier's New England and despoiling surrounding farms, perhaps he would have seen his own people intoxicated with a similar malice.

Anglo-Americans and Creoles responded similarly in many respects to Northern invasion. A discernible difference, however, was the Creoles' refusal to abandon their estates, for they often preferred to remain in Louisiana and take the consequences of war. An occurrence near New Orleans carried the point. A Creole owner watched glumly as the Federal army stripped his great plantation. He might have saved his property by taking General Butler's oath of allegiance, but he would not. He bore the humiliation in silence. Wagons, harness, mules, and horses disappeared. The invaders seized his entire crop, ground it in his sugarhouse, and used his barrels for molasses and hogsheads for sugar, marking on the head of each the letters, "U.S." Finally, the master's 300 slaves left with the liberating soldiers. "The Creole was most completely stripped," declared a witness. "Still he stood in the midst of the ruins, damning Abe Lincoln, and wishing he had eight instead of four sons in the rebel army." [2]

Women frequently remained to manage plantations when planters fled to Texas with the Negroes or marched off with the regiments. These mistresses faced the twofold task of keeping their establishments going without adequate labor and equipment and of dealing with the enemy. In areas free of Union control they contributed heavily in food, clothing, and services to the Confederate army. General Banks paid them the compliment of saying that they had been responsible for bringing on the war and that their encouragement had helped to prolong it. To a

---

[1] De Forest, *Miss Ravenel's Conversion from Secession to Loyalty*, 261.

[2] Hepworth, *Whip, Hoe, and Sword*, 99-100.

plantation woman who petitioned him to make his soldiers stop using such frightful profanity, Banks retorted: "Madam, this war is enough to make any man swear. I swear myself."[1] Plantation wives sometimes exhibited the most fervent patriotism for the Southern cause. The unshakeable spirit of a plantation mistress was revealed in her refusal to take the oath of allegiance to the United States, saying to friends who urged her to do so in order to be spared petty indignities, "No... my husband & children shall never know that mortification."[2]

When it became apparent that the cane country would be invaded, many women and girls, as in other parts of the South, armed themselves for protection against the "hordes of hirelings" from the North. A young Baton Rouge girl almost lost her life when a suitor playfully aimed her pistol at her and accidentally fired.[3]

Plantation women referred the case of the South to the court of heaven. Early in the war one Louisiana woman opined: "I do believe the Lord is on our side. . . . Our sins may be flagrant, and we may need to be scourged with scorpions; but will God permit us to be overwhelmed?" This supplicant possibly was unaware that her enemies prayed to the same deity, though for a different outcome to the war, and she may not have appreciated the familiar apothegm which holds that God favors the side with the heavier artillery. Left without men to defend them, women of the bayou country drew comfort from a rekindled religious faith, which in those anxious days permitted them to sleep the "sleep of the just."[4]

Most women bore the trials of war with admirable fortitude. The steadfastness of Mrs. William T. Palfrey of the Teche country was exemplary. Late in 1862 Palfrey sent his wife and family into Franklin for safekeeping, since the Federal army on the bayou threatened to overrun his plantation, where Confederate troops were encamped. But on January 22, 1863, the wife and children returned to the beleaguered estate, resolved to share the husband's lot for good or bad. "Bad enough at present—God Knows," sighed the planter.[5]

Bayou country women at times possessed as strong a lust for Yankee

---

[1] Merrick, *Old Times in Dixie Land*, 39.
[2] Alfred C. Weeks to John Moore, January 13, 1864, David Weeks and Family Papers.
[3] Dawson, *A Confederate Girl's Diary*, 276.
[4] Merrick, *Old Times in Dixie Land*, 34.
[5] Palfrey Plantation Diary, January 22, 1863.

blood as did the men. A young girl of Baton Rouge was disappointed on one occasion when a battle did not materialize, because she "did want to see [the Yankees] soundly thrashed!" Upon hearing that a Federal steamboat on the Mississippi had been burned, this fiery young Confederate wrote with apparent relish, "They say the shrieks of the men when our hot shells fell among them, and after they were left by their companions to burn, were perfectly appalling." [1]

Hysteria struck feminine hearts at the enemy's approach, a sensation accurately described by one plantation inhabitant, "I write, touch my guitar, talk, pick lint, and pray so rapidly that it is hard to say which is my occupation." [2] But the behavior of plantation girls during the war belied assertions that they were timid and shrinking. They frequently sought excitement at the risk of endangering their lives. While Baton Rouge and the neighboring plantations were under bombardment by Federal gunboats, a number of young ladies rode to the Mississippi in search of diversion. Driving wildly along the levee, they watched the Federal craft *Essex* and the Confederate steamer *Arkansas* jockey for battle position. A group of planters at the waterfront judiciously retired behind the levee, but the irresponsible girls stayed on an exposed point and looked down upon the ill-fated *Arkansas* burning and exploding before them. [3]

The greatest hazard faced by women of the cane plantations was from deserters and guerillas, marauders who took advantage of the absence of men to raid and plunder the countryside. The most lawless area in the state lay near Opelousas, where not even the Union army was able to suppress the desperadoes. An appeal from a "Creole lady" to the men of Opelousas painted this black picture of the situation: "For more than a year past, lawless men have been permitted to band themselves together, and roam at will, ... insulting, chastising, robbing, burning houses, murdering the families of our soldiers; and in some instances despoiling in the most brutal manner, wives, daughters and sisters of that which is dearer than life itself—their honor." The writer begged the men of the town to put an end to these outrages. [4]

Death and injury became commonplace in the cane land during the perilous war years. The Magnolia Plantation overseer commented on

---

[1] Dawson, *A Confederate Girl's Diary*, 340.
[2] *Ibid.*, 336-337.
[3] *Ibid.*, 243.
[4] Opelousas *Courier*, November 12, 1864.

the return of a soldier's body from Tennessee: "Henry Diamond Returned This morning from the army was in the fite at Schilow he has fought Bled & Died for His country."[1] A wounded campaigner arrived at Linwood Plantation near Port Hudson, where his presence electrified the Louisiana girls who had taken refuge there. They buttered the hero's cornbread, carved his mutton, spread his preserves, and sat at his feet, captivated by stories of fighting at Sharpsburg, where he had been struck by a Minié ball.[2]

Plantation families paid for the Civil War with the blood of their sons as well as with their treasure. John Hampden Randolph of Iberville Parish lost his eldest boy during the siege of Vicksburg.[3] In the winter of 1862 William T. Palfrey sadly wrote in his diary, "Received confirmation of the report of my son Edward's death at Vicksburg, in a letter from young Charly Conrad (his cousin), from that place."[4] In June of the next year Lieutenant David Weeks Magill, nephew of Planter John Moore, died in the futile effort to hold the Vicksburg bastion.[5] As the conflict lengthened, the number of widows grew, and the sound of wailing increased. One desolate young woman, whose husband died on the bloody ramparts at Port Hudson, screamed repeatedly, "Why does anybody live when Paul is dead?—dead, dead, forever?"[6]

Under the strain of war, sugar planters sometimes grew bitter toward the conduct of Confederate soldiers. William T. Palfrey penned in his diary a denunciation of a Southerner killed in the Teche country campaign but later the proprietor remorsefully effaced the original entry and replaced it with this penitent explanation: "These erasures were made to obliterate statements which justly reflected on the conduct of an officer...or his ill conduct as I considered it—but having behaved gallantly afterward in other engagements, I do not wish any strictures to remain on records.—He was killed in battle."[7]

War brought great solitude upon most sugar estates. One plantation woman recalled the loneliness that crept over those who remained. "Lacking new books to read and mail to bring us letters, newspapers

---

[1] Magnolia Plantation Journal, August 22, 1862.
[2] Dawson, *A Confederate Girl's Diary*, 252.
[3] Postell, "John Hampden Randolph, a Southern Planter," 115.
[4] Palfrey Plantation Diary, December 13, 1862.
[5] John Moore to General E. Kirby Smith, June 4, 1863, David Weeks and Family Papers.
[6] Merrick, *Old Times in Dixie Land*, 89.
[7] Palfrey Plantation Diary, April 25, 1862.

or magazines," she said, "there yet came into our lives an intenser interest in what was before us so constantly." [1] She referred of course to the ever-present war. Establishments along the Mississippi suffered an unaccustomed isolation. They had always relied upon river packets for intercourse with the outside world, but these facilities were suspended because of war. A plantation mistress declared that the post office might well have been closed, for no mail was received or dispatched. Plantation folk sometimes grew sick and died without nearby relatives and friends knowing anything of their distress until a casual passerby mentioned the event weeks later. [2]

One landowner cried out against the maddening seclusion of his Terrebonne Parish plantations, "Solitude is not good nor proper for man." The proprietor realized that he had erred before the war in sending unmarried sons to manage his sugar estates. "They must at times [have been] very unhappy," said he. "Besides the danger of getting into bad habits." The precise nature of these "bad habits" was not disclosed, but the planter indicated that in the future he intended to make his bachelor sons give up living on the cane plantations. [3]

The desolation of war bore heavily upon the mind of the cane country, and the crumbling, yellowed pages of planters' diaries and journals are filled with their lamentations. In the fall of 1862 A. Franklin Pugh revealed his despondency in saying, "I stay at home now all the time, having very little or nothing to do—but to think over the past and speculate on the future." [4] William J. Minor unfolded the inner emotions of the plantation people as he wrote, "No one who has not been similarly situated can properly understand what I am now suffering all alone. . . ." Never a sound sleeper, and with ruin now staring him in the face, he slept only an hour or two at a time, and found the nights to be terrible ordeals. He wrote in anguish that the death of two of his sons from typhoid fever seemed to have been a blessing. [5] They were spared the nightmare of defeat.

In the fall of 1863 Minor cast the sugar planters' horoscope of gloom and woe: "If the war continues twelve months longer, all negro men of any value will be taken, the women & children will be left, for their

---

[1] Merrick, *Old Times in Dixie Land*, 47.
[2] Ripley, *From Flag to Flag*, 44.
[3] Minor Plantation Diary (1863), February 5.
[4] Pugh Plantation Diary, November 26, 1862.
[5] Minor Plantation Diary (1863), March 2, May 20.

masters to maintain, which they can not do.—The owners of the soil will make nothing, the lands will be sold for taxes, & bot in by Northern men, & the original owners will be made beggars—This is the result of Secession & abolitionism.—Was there ever such folly since the world began—." [1]

William T. Palfrey, a cultivator whose fiery eloquence only three short years before had helped to whip up fighting spirit in St. Mary Parish, cursed his fate and the men whom he believed to be the architects of his misfortune. In the winter of 1863 he asserted that from a condition of comfort and abundance he had been reduced by war to one of hardship and want. He hoped the Devil would take both abolitionists and fire eaters, who, he charged, had shown the "white feather, and with few exceptions, [had] run away." In the spring of the next year he shaped a classic summary of the troubles that had come upon the people of the sugar land: "The days (emphatically days of darkness & gloom) succeed each other bringing nothing but despondency with regard to the future— Our beautiful Parish is laid waste & is likely to become a desert— Plantations abandoned fences & buildings destroyed, mules, horses & cattle driven off by the federals, the negroes conscripted into the army or wandering about without employment or support, & stealing for a living —Those who remain are insolent & refractory, and in domestic, family arrangements the few who continue with their owners are more trouble & vexation than they are of use.—Their laziness & impertinence is beyond belief.—There can be no crop made in the country and of course starvation will be the dreadful consequence.—All this is fearful to consider, and if indiscriminate plunder & massacre do not supervene we may be considered lucky.—The Lord help us.—Such is war, civil war." [2]

William J. Minor wrote on April 19, 1865, a Unionist planter's reaction to the last and most dramatic bloodshed of the long and fearful contest: "Stephen came out to day from the city & brot the terrible news that Mr. Lincoln had been assassinated in Fords Theatre in Washington by one Wilks Booth.... This is one of the most extra-ordinary occurrences in the history of the world, & is in my... judgment one of the greatest misfortunes that could have befallen the country.—I had, since the fall of Richmond, & the surrender of Lee... begun to admit the hope of an

---

[1] Minor Plantation Diary (1863-1868), September 29, 1863.
[2] Palfrey Plantation Diary, January 22, 1863, March 16, 1864.

early peace. ... At one time, I considered Mr. Seward the ablest man in Mr. Lincoln's government—Some time since I came to the conclusion that Mr. L. Himself was the ablest & the most conservative man in the Washington Government.—His death is therefore, in my opinion, a great loss to the whole country & especially to the South—as from him, we had a right to expect better terms of peace than from any one else at all likely to come into power.—Oh! my poor country—What have you yet to Suffer." [1]

Confederate victories early in the war sent a wave of elation through the bayou land, but plantation inhabitants soon were sobered by death notices of sons, husbands, and sweethearts. Four years of slaughter and destruction brought planters from the dawn of exultation to the black night of despair.

---

[1] Minor Plantation Diary (1863-1868), April 19, 1865.

CHAPTER X

FROLICS AND FRIVOLITIES

War blighted the colorful social life of many families in the sugar land. Plantation daughters were lonely after planters' sons marched away to the armies, while wartime shortages greatly reduced the sumptuousness of balls and dinners. Casualty lists from the fighting front shattered many homes and brushed away all thoughts of gaiety. Nevertheless, life and play went on, even in the midst of the holocaust. Encompassed by the hazards of war and the stringencies and uncertainties of hostile occupation, many inhabitants of the sugar estates still found amusements to suit their tastes and situations.

Dancing remained a favorite among plantation pastimes. On a sugar establishment near Port Hudson, pretty young refugees from plantations then in Federal hands farther down the river swirled merrily with Confederate officers from nearby camps. A tall, supple artillery lieutenant, putting his "best foot forward," and eminently aware of his charms, left a striking impression on one of the girls. Flirting became the order of the day as these mettlesome youths, sublimely oblivious of the tragedy that soon would engulf them, swung across the floor in rhythm to the tunes of a piano.[1]

Characteristics of wartime parties were excitement, deprivation, and sometimes danger. A dinner party on a Mississippi River plantation demonstrated the violent days that had come upon the cane land. The hostess was a young widow whose husband had died on the earthworks at Port Hudson, and who sought to forget her sorrow by taking a gay social fling. The plantation was abandoned except for the bereaved mistress, her aunt, and a few household servants. All Confederate soldiers home on furlough, who were old friends of the family, were invited. Girls from neighboring plantations, wearing an odd assortment of clothes, came by any available transportation. Some rode in men's saddles, others rode double, and many were astride mules. One beauty wore a jacket made from an old piano cover.

The soldiers and ladies danced and romped in the parlor to the jangle of an untuned piano. After hours of exaggerated hilarity they sat down

---

[1] Dawson, *A Confederate Girl's Diary*, 313.

to the resourceful hostess' dinner of ham and roast turkey. Dessert consisted of cornmeal poundcake and eggnog, a beverage sharpened with a generous portion of "crude and fiery rum" made from plantation molasses. The girls did not appreciate this throat-burning delicacy, but the soldiers drank freely, repeating the saying of the governor of South Carolina, "It is a long time between drinks." According to one account, the plantation had never seen a merrier day. The party ended as abruptly as a bugle call, thrown into consternation by the appearance of an enemy gunboat on the river. The hostess scooped up and hid the family silver; Confederate soldiers vanished miraculously; and girls took an undignified retreat astride their lowly mules.[1]

Where plantations were still in operation, sugarhouse frolics continued to be a choice form of entertainment. The presence of fun-loving Southern soldiers lent glamour to these parties in areas not overrun by Northern troops. On the second night of cane grinding at Linwood Plantation near Port Hudson the owner suggested that the girls and their uniformed beaux visit the sugarhouse. At ten o'clock a group of about twenty strolled through the fall moonlight to the busy establishment. The revelers stopped to warm themselves and chat at the great furnace. The inside of the sugarhouse was illuminated by "Confederate gas"—pine torches—which shed a soft light over the scene. From room to room wandered the happy party. At one point the girls grasped the syrup ladles from the Negroes, dipping up sugary liquid and eating it with relish, while others contented themselves with chewing sugar cane under the pine torches.

Someone suggested a game of "Puss wants a corner." "Such racing for corners!" wrote a participant. "Such scuffles among the gentlemen! Such confusion among the girls when, springing forward for a place, we would find it already occupied." Dignity retreated in the face of such merriment, and the entire group responded like children. The owner enjoyed the fun as much as did the young people, encouraging them in their pranks. Some of the Confederate officers entered the game with gusto, while others disapproved and sulked. Some appeared "timidly foolish and half afraid of [the] wild sport." Men who a few weeks later would distinguish themselves for gallantry in the carnage of Port Hudson were unassertive in the presence of cavorting plantation belles.

When the furious exercise of "Puss wants a corner" subsided, the young

---

[1] Merrick, *Old Times in Dixie Land*, 95-99.

people sat down to a more sedate form of entertainment. A game of "forfeits" provided fun, excitement, and gay absurdity. One lieutenant unknowingly sentenced himself to ride a barrel. A young lady was forced to make a love speech to her escort. Another had to make "a declaration" to one of the officers. Then came more cane chewing and conversation until at twelve o'clock orders were given to retire.[1]

The presence of Confederate troops in parts of the cane country enlivened immensely the social life of plantations on which they stopped. In August of 1862 the crew of the sunken Confederate gunboat *Arkansas* appeared at an estate near Baton Rouge. The women could not ask them in, since the plantation owner was on parole, but the proprietor's daughter hinted that if sailors "chose to order," they could do as they pleased, "as women could not resist armed men!" The commander "chose to order," and the Confederates took over the sugarhouse, commandeered food, and flirted openly with the girls. Each eager young lady appropriated an officer, naming him Miriam's, Ginnie's, or Sarah's, as though he belonged to her, and the robust young Rebels engaged in the pleasantry of planning an attack on the Yankees in Baton Rouge. The commander of the *Arkansas* would lead the fleet, according to this mock strategy, and a battalion of mettlesome girls would assault the enemy from the rear. The next day as the men departed, the young women further endeared themselves by passing out bottles of gin.[2]

Plantation daughters courted and played for months with the Confederates, who, like the soldiers of Mrs. Mary Boykin Chesnut's famous Civil War diary, danced to the fiddle or piano at the sugar establishments only to do the *danse macabre* in the rifle pits of Port Hudson later. A favorite pastime was chewing sugar cane. One bashful Tennessee campaigner who had never engaged in this pleasantry hung back while the group indulged. Finally he was persuaded to participate, and once instructed "he got on remarkably well, and ate it in a civilized manner, considering it was a first attempt."[3]

The appearance of Southern soldiers at a mansion invariably put the girls into a dither. At dusk one evening a group of young ladies sat in their bedroom playing cards when a number of officers arrived at the house. Down went the cards, and the girls were instantly in a mad scramble for their best clothes. One belle wondered whether soldiers

---

[1] Dawson, *A Confederate Girl's Diary*, 272-274.
[2] *Ibid.*, 155-156.
[3] *Ibid.*, 265.

were worth all the trouble, but the answer to that question seems always to have been in the affirmative. Another beauty even sprang from the sickbed, dressing frantically as though she had never had a pain, and thereby demonstrating that the approach of handsome Confederates could at times have a remarkable therapeutic value for girls of the cane country.[1]

Planters often invited Confederate officers to dine in their homes. On August 29, 1862, Texas troopers were guests for dinner at Bayside Plantation on the Teche.[2] A Union lieutenant in General Banks' army wrote from near Opelousas in 1863 of almost capturing a group of Southern officers at a planter's table. The writer stopped for the night at a recently deserted plantation mansion. The Negroes who remained on the place said that the owner was an officer in the Confederate army and stated that the master and several fellow officers were at the table when the Federal cavalry came into sight. They fled hurriedly, leaving the meal uneaten.[3]

The conviviality of plantation inhabitants once induced a Southern general to relax his customary discipline. In the spring of 1863 General Franklin Gardner—commander of Port Hudson—dined on a nearby plantation, where he soon struck up a conversation with the girls. One of them gently reproached him for refusing to permit his young officers to pay calls at the plantation, whereupon the gallant general promised her that he would grant passes to any gentlemen who signified they were visiting that particular place.[4]

A delightful association sprang up between the plantation folk of Pointe Coupee Parish and Confederate soldiers encamped in the area. Officers frequently dined in the mansions, where every family had stored away for special occasions small quantities of wine, tea, and coffee. General Richard Taylor once sat at the table of a plantation family and not too tactfully exclaimed while sipping champagne, "I'm astonished, madam, that in these times you can be living in such luxury." The mistress hastened to explain that it was her daughter's birthday, for which they had long hoarded the precious beverage, and in honor of which

---

[1] *Ibid.*, 321, 331.

[2] Bayside Plantation Journal, August 29, 1862.

[3] Root (ed.), "Private Journal of William H. Root, Second Lieutenant, Seventy-fifth New York Volunteers, April 1-June 14, 1863," introduction by Walter Prichard, *Louisiana Historical Quarterly*, XIX (July, 1936), 644-645.

[4] Dawson, *A Confederate Girl's Diary*, 346.

the last bottle had been opened. On one occasion Confederate General Charles Polignac dined at the same house, and while eating green peas and roast lamb inquired whether the peas were grown under glass. "Look at my broken windows, all over the house," the hostess shot back wittily. "And tell whether I can raise peas under glass when we can't keep ourselves under it!" [1]

Plantation inhabitants occasionally enjoyed visits to Confederate camps. In September of 1862 citizens near Port Hudson called upon friends and relatives there. The visitors traveled in "Confederate carriages," which were rough wagons drawn by mules. Self-conscious troops went through their paces in review before excited parents and sweethearts. Afterward the young ladies and their escorts inspected long rows of tents, which brought to mind similar camps in Virginia and Tennessee where other close friends and relatives were stationed. A feminine observer commented: "Altogether it was a very pretty picture; but poor men! how can they be happy in those tents?" In October a "little cavalcade" of plantation folk, including a number of spirited girls, journeyed to Port Hudson for a look at the fortifications. They made a pleasant excursion of the affair, chatting and flirting with the soldiers. Guns frowning from the bluffs overlooking the Mississippi were declared invincible by these impressionable young women, who found the "water battery," an installation of artillery concealed by a cluster of trees at the river's edge, especially formidable. The party rode through great encampments of gaping troops and along endless rows of rifle pits, and afterward pronounced the inspection an overwhelming success. [2]

Many customary social events continued despite the stern aspect of the times. In some areas plantation families still went to church on Sundays, although in others the churches were closed. Deprivations of war did not altogether rob weddings of their festive nature. In May of 1864 a Bayou Teche planter attended the nuptials of two of his young friends and pronounced the host's dinner excellent. [3]

Funerals continued to draw the planters' interest. In June of 1862 a St. Mary Parish landowner went to a funeral and was impressed by the unusually large procession to the grave. [4] A year later a prominent cane grower was present at the funeral of an acquaintance and noted that the

---

[1] Merrick, *Old Times in Dixie Land*, 73-74.
[2] Dawson, *A Confederate Girl's Diary*, 235, 246-247.
[3] Bayside Plantation Journal, May 15, 1864.
[4] *Ibid.*, June 24, 1862.

widow fainted at the tomb.[1] In October of 1863 this proprietor attended a friend's funeral, where in the absence of a minister he was called upon to read the service, which he did according to the Episcopal ceremony. Unprepared and taken by surprise, the planter was embarrassed, but he chuckled at a humorous thrust by the plantation Negroes to the effect that they did not see how a horse racer could be a preacher.[2]

Wartime cares did not always obliterate the amenities of graceful living. Austerities failed to stop planters from drinking to the health of friends and relatives on their birthdays. A great landowner dined frequently with his associates, and on at least one occasion enjoyed the delicacy of a quantity of fish caught in a crevasse in the levee. As late as the fall of 1863 he and his friends were able to obtain food and wines which even this finished connoisseur pronounced excellent.[3]

Innumerable small amusements helped to make life bearable in the days of mental stress and material shortages. For some sugar land inhabitants reading was a favorite diversion. In the fall of 1862 a young woman on a plantation near Port Hudson read, among other publications, Abbot's *Napoleon* and Dumas' *Memoires*. Another choice pastime was pulling molasses candy, a sticky but appetizing sport that filled many a long evening in the bayou country.[4]

Simple and inexpensive pleasures took on added significance. Plantation folk sometimes enjoyed the luxury of taking strolls and cart rides at sundown. One evening, as a group of young ladies left for a ride, the elder women of the place cautioned them to be careful of the mud, reminding them that soap was $1.50 a bar and starch $1.00 a pound. Skirts were lifted to avoid soiling. "You can imagine how high [they were elevated]," wrote a member of the party, "when I tell you my answer to a question as to whether [another girl's skirts] were in danger of touching the mud." The reply, considered exquisitely risqué for the times, was, "Not unless you sit down."[5]

A headstrong and flighty plantation belle engaged in a heartless trick upon a suitor who was seriously in love with her. She played a game of cards with him, in which she wagered herself and lost. To her, the whole affair was a huge joke; but the man, who was quite sincere,

---

[1] Minor Plantation Diary (1863), April 25.
[2] Minor Plantation Diary (1863-1868), October 1, 1863.
[3] Minor Plantation Diary (1863), September 13.
[4] Dawson, *A Confederate Girl's Diary*, 244, 268.
[5] *Ibid.*, 181.

notified all of his friends that he was to be married and arranged for a minister to perform the ceremony. At the last moment the brutal hoax was exposed to the incredulous minister and group of witnesses. The victim was desolated but powerless to remedy the situation.[1]

Folk of the sugar land sometimes fraternized socially with enemy soldiers. Young women of Pointe Coupee Parish were furious that a feminine acquaintance should be so bold as to ride with Northern officers. "Shame on her!" stormed a patriotic accuser.[2] Citizens of Baton Rouge entertained Union soldiers in their homes. A Northern trooper stationed in the capital city declared that the people were Rebel to the core, but that they were refined and pleasant, and that a number of young Federal officers had calling acquaintances with the ladies of Baton Rouge families.[3]

Many girls in and around Plaquemine across the Mississippi from Baton Rouge found the company of Northern boys to their taste and consorted openly with them. The Federals were dined and entertained. A Northern campaigner was amazed to see girls who had sung the *Bonnie Blue Flag* and *Maryland, My Maryland* rationalizing their blushes with the argument that Ohio soldiers were not Yankees, but Western people like themselves. When the Union regiment was transferred to another location, the girls wept bitterly and waved handkerchiefs as their new-found beaux marched away.[4]

Planters sometimes wined and dined with Federal soldiers. A. Franklin Pugh frequently invited Union officers to dinner. On August 27, 1864, he gave a dinner party for officers stationed at Paincourtville on Bayou Lafourche. A few days later the local provost marshal, the post commander, and the colonel of the regiment enjoyed Pugh's hospitality.[5] In this way, ties of friendship were cemented with Federal officials whose favors proprietors so desperately needed.

Invading Federals sometimes got in on the jollity of sugarhouse parties. In December of 1864 a Rhode Island cavalryman wrote from Napoleonville on Bayou Lafourche that the sugar mills in that area were in full operation. A proprietress whom the soldier knew planned to close

---

[1] *Ibid.*, 291-294.
[2] Merrick, *Old Times in Dixie Land*, 40.
[3] Clark, *Life in the Middle West*, 115.
[4] Mason, *The Forty-second Ohio Infantry*, 247.
[5] Lathrop, "The Pugh Plantations, 1860-1865; a Study of Life in Lower Louisiana," 353-354.

down her establishment within the next few days, and he was looking forward to an old-time "blow out."[1]

Plantations belonging to Unionists frequently were the setting for dances and parties attended by Federal officers. The famous novelist, George Washington Cable, set down in fiction a vivid picture of one of these affairs. The Gilmer sisters, daughters of a Unionist planter, arranged the party. A few non-Unionist plantation girls attended, according to the author, because this was their way of saving house and home for their brothers, who would return when the Yankees were "purged out of the land."

Cable's description of the ball preserved the flavor of the times. While some of the guests ate cake and custard and sipped punch in the dining room, others swirled to the music of a black plantation fiddler. Ladies and gentlemen counted off by two's, while the Negro musician coaxed lively tunes from his instrument and exultantly shouted directions:

> O ladies ramble in,
>   Whilst de beaux ramble out,
> For to quile (coil) dat golden chain.
>   My Lawdy! it's a sin
>   Fo' a fidleh not to shout!
> Miss Charlotte's a-comin' down de lane![2]

Inhabitants of the cane plantations knew the fury of war and the humiliation of defeat. Their lot was often sorrowful. They were able, however, to preserve a sense of humor and to adjust their lives to the bleak stringencies of the times. Even the enemy succumbed to the delights of a sugarhouse party, a dance, or a tasty dinner. The love of play and gaiety for which the sugar land was famous survived the shock of war, and in this resilience lay the people's salvation.

---

[1] New Orleans *Daily True Delta*, December 11, 1864.
[2] George Washington Cable, *The Cavalier* (New York, 1910), 213-214.

CHAPTER XI

EPILOGUE

War brought the Louisiana sugar industry to the brink of extinction. The closest estimates of the value of sugar property in 1861 ran to almost $200,000,000; four years later, with slaves freed, sugarhouses ruined or severely damaged, livestock confiscated, and land prices vastly depreciated, the industry was worth hardly more than one eighth of that figure.[1]

The most revolutionary change wrought by the conflict was the transition from slave to free labor, for the return of peace found proprietors and freedmen floundering in a desperate effort to adjust to the new order. Planters still looked askance at the payment of wages to Negroes, while the blacks were for a long period shiftless and undependable. Many landowners sought immigrant labor, but all attempts to bring in workers from the North, from Europe, and from China met with disappointment, since the cane growers desired peasants to till their estates and refused to break them up into small farms.[2]

In spite of the planters' prejudice and the Negroes' desire to possess farms of their own, the inevitable solution to this vexing problem lay in free black labor, for the proprietors had fields that they themselves could not tend, while on every hand were thousands of freedmen, without land or money. Time passed; the Negroes settled to the task of making a living; and the attitude of the whites gradually softened. Immediately after the war sugar producers almost universally condemned free labor, but in less than a decade many of them felt that freedmen could be relied upon to man the fields and sugarhouses. In 1875 Charles Nordhoff, an observant Northerner who traveled the South, wrote: "The planters,

---

[1] Sitterson, *Sugar Country*, 226. By adding the value of growing cane destroyed, a contemporary authority on the sugar industry calculated its losses at $199,124,000. Latham, *Black and White*, 171.

[2] Contemporary newspapers and travel accounts abound in articles on Louisiana immigration efforts. See, for example, Opelousas *Courier*, December 9, 1865; New Orleans *Daily Southern Star*, December 29, 1865; West Baton Rouge [Port Allen] *Sugar Planter*, February 10, 1866; Thibodaux *Sentinel*, June 1, 1867; Plaquemine *Iberville South*, April 13, 1864; Donaldsonville *Chief*, December 16, 1871; Charles W. Dilke, *Greater Britain; a Record of Travel in English-Speaking Countries, during 1866-67* (Philadelphia, 1869), 22; and Daniel Dennett, *Louisiana as It Is; Its Topography and Material Resources* (New Orleans, 1876), 36.

without exception, so far as I have heard them speak, are thoroughly satisfied with the colored man as a laborer. I do not mean to say that they have no fault to find; but they say that the negroes are orderly, docile, faithful to their engagements, steady laborers in the field, readily submitting to directions and instructions, and easily managed and made contented. ... All is summed up in the phrase I most frequently heard used, 'We have the best laboring class in the world.' "[1] Here was a clear indication of a meeting of Southern and Northern minds as to the role of the Negro in the New South.

The labor pattern that emerged in the sugar land was that of hiring workers by the month. In most cases, laborers continued to live in cabins owned by the planters—the post-war counterpart of the slave quarters. Because of the great expense of sugar-making machinery and the prevailing custom whereby each producer had his own sugarhouse, neither renting nor share-cropping became as popular as in cotton agriculture.

To many observers the great sugar estates appeared to be breaking up into small farms during the years immediately after the struggle, but actually this did not happen on a large scale, for the plantation system survived the impact of war and emancipation.[2] The same factors that prevented widespread development of the tenant plan—high-priced apparatus and the requirement that each cane grower process his own crop—deterred the growth of a small-farm economy, and even today the large plantation still dominates the cane culture.[3]

Although the sugar estates generally remained intact, ownership shifted greatly during the post-war era. Much capital was needed to mend the wounds of the industry, and many original landowners lacked sufficient money to get back into operation. As a result, cane land depreciated at alarming rate. Mortgages were foreclosed daily, and by 1867 land had dropped to less than one fourth of its previous value. Places that in normal times would have brought $150,000 sold for scarcely more than $30,000.[4] During the 1870's the Southern Land Company, a Louisiana real estate firm, advertised scores of sugar plantations for sale at less than the original cost of their houses and equipment.[5]

---

[1] Charles Nordhoff, *The Cotton States in the Spring and Summer of 1875* (New York, 1876), 56.

[2] Shugg, *Origins of Class Struggle in Louisiana*, 241.

[3] Sitterson, *Sugar Country*, 388. By 1910 there were about 4,000 white tenants growing sugar in Louisiana. *Ibid.*, 314.

[4] *De Bow's Review*, III, N. S. (March, 1867), 308.

[5] Dennett, *Louisiana as It Is*, 272.

EPILOGUE   139

Cheap land invited men with money—merchants and bankers of all sections—to invest in what looked like certain prosperity, and many old sugar planters lost their estates by foreclosure, or sold them to avoid this fate. Everywhere cane establishments fell to speculators at incredibly low figures. [1] One student of the post-war Louisiana agricultural pattern estimates that after 1870 at least half of the planters were either of Northern birth or were backed by Northern money. [2]

During the decades after the war, vitality gradually returned to the cane industry, but the high cost of sugar machinery made recovery painfully slow as compared with that of cotton, which within five years was almost back to normal. [3] Not until 1893 did sugar production equal the 1862 output. [4] As the complexity and cost of apparatus soared, a gradual divorcement of sugar agriculture and manufacture occurred, and the number of sugarhouses decreased, with the less affluent cultivators turning exclusively to planting. But the shift was slow, and as late as 1879 there were 1,130 sugarhouses still in operation. [5] By the twentieth century, however, the process was well along; large planters generally owned the mills, to which less extensive producers brought their cane for sale. Today only about 60 sugarhouses remain of the 1,291 in production on the eve of the Civil War. [6]

Ultimately the cane industry regained its economic strength, but the soul was gone from the old sugar civilization. Great numbers of plantations after the war belonged to Northern entrepreneurs and to banks and corporations. [7] The plantation ideal ceased to predominate, as bankers, merchants, and business enterprisers replaced landed proprietors in the public imagination, while emancipation of the slaves reduced the sugar growers' old sense of patriarchal omnipotence. Today three landmarks of the ante-bellum sugar plantations remain: the broad, canal-gridded cane fields; occasional sugarhouses, infinitely more elaborate than of old; and the great, proud mansions—ghosts along the waters.

---

[1] West Baton Rouge [Port Allen] *Sugar Planter*, December 12, 1868; Nordhoff, *The Cotton States in the Spring and Summer of 1875*, 69; and John T. Trowbridge, *The South; a Tour of Its Battlefields and Ruined Cities* (Hartford, 1866), 411.

[2] Shugg, *Origins of Class Struggle in Louisiana*, 248.

[3] Somers, *The Southern States since the War*, 199.

[4] Alcée Bouchereau, *Statement of the Sugar and Rice Crops Made in Louisiana, 1893-1894* (New Orleans, 1894), 44a. Statements were issued annually.

[5] Bouchereau, *Statement of the Sugar and Rice Crops Made in Louisiana, 1878-1879*, 104.

[6] Sitterson, *Sugar Country*, 388.

[7] Shugg, *Origins of Class Struggle in Louisiana*, 248.

BIBLIOGRAPHY

MANUSCRIPTS

Bayside Plantation Journal, microfilm copy in possession of author, of original in Southern Historical Collection, University of North Carolina Library, Chapel Hill.
Andrew E. Crane Papers, Department of Archives, Louisiana State University, Baton Rouge.
Magnolia Plantation Journal (1852-1862), microfilm copy and original in Southern Historical Collection, University of North Carolina Library.
Charles Mathews and Family Papers, Department of Archives, Louisiana State University.
William J. Minor and Family Papers, Department of Archives, Louisiana State University. Five separate volumes of the William J. Minor Plantation Diary (1847-1870) in this collection and cited in this study include entries dated 1861-1862, 1861-1865, 1861-1868, 1863, and 1863-1868.
Thomas O. Moore Papers, Department of Archives, Louisiana State University.
Robert Newell Papers, Department of Archives, Louisiana State University.
William T. Palfrey Plantation Diary (1842-1895), Department of Archives, Louisiana State University.
A. Franklin Pugh Plantation Diary (1850, 1859-1863), Department of Archives, Louisiana State University.
John Hampden Randolph and Family Papers, Department of Archives, Louisiana State University.
St. Charles Parish Police Jury Minutes, transcription in Department of Archives, Louisiana State University, of original in St. Charles Parish courthouse, Hahnville, Louisiana.
United States Census Returns, 1860, Schedule IV, Agriculture, microfilm copy in Hill Memorial Library, Louisiana State University, of original in Duke University Library, Durham.
David Weeks and Family Papers, Department of Archives, Louisiana State University. Included is the John Moore Plantation Journal (1847-1867) cited in this study.

PUBLIC DOCUMENTS

Historical Records Survey, *Transcriptions of Parish Records of Louisiana; Number 24, Iberville Parish (Plaquemine), Series I, Police Jury Minutes*, Baton Rouge, April, 1940-March, 1942.
——, *Transcriptions of Parish Records of Louisiana; Number 26, Jefferson Parish (Gretna), Series I, Police Jury Minutes*, Baton Rouge, June, 1939-February, 1941.
The War of the Rebellion; a Compilation of the Official Records of the Union and Confederate Armies, 128 vols., Washington, 1880-1901.

NEWSPAPERS AND PERIODICAL

De Bow's Review, New Orleans, 1860-1867.
Donaldsonville *Chief*, 1871.
New Orleans *Bee*, 1863.
New Orleans *Daily Crescent*, 1860-1865.
New Orleans *Daily Picayune*, 1862-1866.
New Orleans *Daily Southern Star*, 1865.

New Orleans *Daily True Delta*, 1861-1866.
New Orleans *Era*, 1863.
New Orleans *Price-Current*, 1864.
New Orleans *States*, 1925.
New Orleans *Times*, 1863-1865.
Opelousas *Courier*, 1862-1864.
Plaquemine *Iberville South*, 1867.
Thibodaux *Sentinel*, 1867.
West Baton Rouge [Port Allen] *Sugar Planter*, 1866-1867.

PUBLISHED DIARIES, MEMOIRS, AND CONTEMPORARY ACCOUNTS

Banks, Nathaniel P., *Emancipated Labor in Louisiana*, New York, 1864.
Bentley, William H., *History of the Seventy-seventh Illinois Volunteer Infantry*, Peoria, 1883.
Bouchereau, Alcée, *Statement of the Sugar and Rice Crops Made in Louisiana, 1878-1879*, New Orleans, 1879. Statements were issued annually.
Butler, Benjamin F., *Autobiography and Personal Reminiscences of Major-General Benjamin F. Butler; Butler's Book*, Boston, 1892.
———, *Character and Results of the War; How to Prosecute It and How to End It*, Philadelphia, 1863.
Calvert, Henry Murray, *Reminiscences of a Boy in Blue, 1862-1865*, New York, 1920.
Champomier, P. A., *Statement of the Sugar Crop Made in Louisiana in 1861-1862*, New Orleans, 1862. Statements were issued annually.
Clark, J. S., *Life in the Middle West*, Chicago, 1916.
Corsan, W. C., *Two Months in the Confederate States, Including a Visit to New Orleans under the Domination of General Butler*, London, 1863.
Dawson, Sarah Morgan, *A Confederate Girl's Diary*, New York, 1913.
De Forest, John W., *A Volunteer's Adventures; a Union Captain's Record of the Civil War*, New Haven, 1946.
Dennett, Daniel, *Louisiana as It Is; Its Topography and Material Resources*, New Orleans, 1876.
Dilke, Charles W., *Greater Britain; a Record of Travel in English-Speaking Countries, during 1866-67*, Philadelphia, 1869.
Duganne, Alexander J. H., *Camps and Prisons; Twenty Months in the Department of the Gulf*, New York, 1865.
Fearn, Frances (ed.), *Diary of a Refugee*, New York, 1910.
Flinn, Frank M., *Campaigning with Banks in Louisiana*, Lynn, Massachusetts, 1887.
Fowler, William, *Memorials of William Fowler*, New York, 1875.
Fremantle, A. J., *Three Months in the Southern States; April-June, 1863*, New York, 1864.
Gould, John M., *History of the First- Tenth- Twenty-ninth Maine Regiment*, Portland, 1871.
Hepworth, George Hughes, *The Whip, Hoe, and Sword; or the Gulf Department in '63*, Boston, 1864.
Johns, Henry T., *Life with the Forty-ninth Massachusetts Volunteers*, Pittsfield, Massachusetts, 1864.
Johnson, Charles B., *Muskets and Medicine; or Army Life in the Sixties*, Philadelphia, 1917.
Latham, Henry, *Black and White; a Journal of a Three Month's Tour in the United States*, London, 1867.
Lloyd, Caroline (ed.), *A Memorial of Lieutenant Daniel Perkins Dewey, of the Twenty-fifth Regiment, Connecticut Volunteers*, Hartford, 1864.

Mackie, John M., *From Cape Cod to Dixie and the Tropics*, New York, 1864.
Marshall, Albert O., *Army Life; from a Soldier's Journal*, Joliet, 1884.
Marshall, Jessie A. (ed.), *Private and Official Correspondence of General Benjamin F. Butler during the Period of the Civil War*, 5 vols., Norwood, Massachusetts, 1917.
Mason, Frank H., *The Forty-second Ohio Infantry; a History of the Organization and Services of That Regiment in the War of the Rebellion*, Cleveland, 1876.
Merrick, Caroline E., *Old Times in Dixie Land; a Southern Matron's Memories*, New York, 1901.
Newsome, E., *Experience in the War of the Great Rebellion*, Carbondale, Illinois, 1879.
Nordhoff, Charles, *The Cotton States in the Spring and Summer of 1875*, New York, 1876.
Nott, Charles C., *Sketches of the War*, New York, 1865.
Olmsted, Frederick Law, *A Journey in the Seaboard Slave States in the Years 1853-1854, with Remarks on Their Economy*, New York, 1856.
Powers, George W., *The Story of the Thirty-eighth Regiment of Massachusetts Volunteers*, Cambridge, 1866.
Ripley, Eliza McHatton, *From Flag to Flag; a Woman's Adventures and Experiences in the South during the War, in Mexico, and in Cuba*, New York, 1889.
Russell, William Howard, *My Diary North and South*, Boston, 1863.
Smith, George G., *Leaves from a Soldier's Diary; the Personal Record of Lieutenant George G. Smith, First Louisiana Regiment, Infantry Volunteers*, Putnam, Connecticut, 1906.
Somers, Robert, *The Southern States since the War*, New York, 1871.
Stevenson, Benjamin Franklin, *Letters from the Army*, Cincinnati, 1864.
Taylor, Richard, *Destruction and Reconstruction; Personal Experiences of the Late War*, New York, 1879.
Torrey, Rodney W., *War Diary of Rodney W. Torrey, 1862-1863*, n.p., n.d.
Trowbridge, John T., *The South; a Tour of Its Battlefields and Ruined Cities*, Hartford, 1866.
Tunnard, William H., *A Southern Record; the History of the Third Regiment Louisiana Infantry*, Baton Rouge, 1866.
Van Alstyne, Lawrence, *Diary of an Enlisted Man*, New Haven, 1910.
Watson, William, *Life in the Confederate Army; Being the Observations and Experiences of an Alien in the South during the American Civil War*, London, 1887.
Yeatman, James E., *Suggestions of a Plan of Organization for Freed Labor*, St. Louis, 1864.

SECONDARY WORKS

Adams, Henry, *The Education of Henry Adams*, New York, 1931.
Bragg, Jefferson Davis, *Louisiana in the Confederacy*, Baton Rouge, 1941.
Cable, George Washington, *The Cavalier*, New York, 1910.
Caskey, Willie Malvin, *Secession and Restoration of Louisiana*, Baton Rouge, 1938.
Davis, Edwin Adams, *Plantation Life in the Florida Parishes of Louisiana, 1836-1846, as Reflected in the Diary of Bennet H. Barrow*, New York, 1943.
De Forest, John W., *Miss Ravenel's Conversion from Secession to Loyalty*, New York, 1939.
Dorsey, Sarah Anne, *Recollections of Henry Watkins Allen, Brigadier-General Confederate States Army, Ex-Governor of Louisiana*, New York, 1866.
Ficklen, John Rose, *History of Reconstruction in Louisiana through 1868*, Baltimore, 1910.
Gray, Lewis C., *History of Agriculture in the Southern United States to 1860*, 2 vols., Washington, 1933.

Kassel, Charles, *The Labor System of General Banks; a Lost Episode of Civil War History*, n.p., n.d.
May, Thomas P., *The Earl of Mayfield*, Philadelphia, 1880.
Moody, V. Alton, *Slavery on Louisiana Sugar Plantations*, New Orleans, 1924.
Parton, James, *General Butler in New Orleans; Being a History of the Administration of the Department of the Gulf in the Year 1862*, New York, 1864.
Peirce, Paul S., *The Freedmen's Bureau*, Iowa City, 1904.
Phillips, Ulrich B., *American Negro Slavery; a Survey of the Supply, Employment and Control of Negro Labor as Determined by the Plantation Regime*, New York, 1918.
——, *Life and Labor in the Old South*, Boston, 1929.
Randall, James G., *The Civil War and Reconstruction*, New York, 1937.
Shugg, Roger W., *Origins of Class Struggle in Louisiana; a Social History of White Farmers and Laborers during Slavery and after, 1840-1875*, Baton Rouge, 1939.
Sitterson, J. Carlyle, *Sugar Country; the Cane Industry in the South*, Lexington, 1953.
Wiley, Bell I., *Southern Negroes, 1861-1865*, New Haven, 1938.
Work Projects Administration, *Louisiana; a Guide to the State*, New York, 1941.

ARTICLES

Butler, Louise, "The Louisiana Planter and His Home," *Louisiana Historical Quarterly* (New Orleans), X (July, 1927), 271-279.
Greer, James K., "Louisiana Politics, 1845-1861," *Louisiana Historical Quarterly*, XIII (October, 1930), 617-654.
Kendall, Lane C., "The Interregnum in Louisiana in 1861," *Louisiana Historical Quarterly*, XVI (July, 1933), 374-408.
Laurent, Lubin F., "History of St. John the Baptist Parish," *Louisiana Historical Quarterly*, VII (April, 1924), 316-331.
Prichard, Walter, "The Effects of the Civil War on the Louisiana Sugar Industry," *Journal of Southern History* (Baton Rouge, Lexington), V (August, 1939), 315-332.
——, "A Louisiana Sugar Plantation under the Slavery Regime," *Mississippi Valley Historical Review* (Cedar Rapids), XIX (September, 1927), 168-178.
Richardson, Frank L., "War as I Saw It," *Louisiana Historical Quarterly*, VI (April, 1923), 86-106.
Root, L. Carroll (ed.), "Private Journal of William H. Root, Second Lieutenant, Seventy-fifth New York Volunteers, April 1-June 14, 1863," introduction by Walter Prichard, *Louisiana Historical Quarterly*, XIX (July, 1936), 635-667.
Sitterson, J. Carlyle, "The McCollams; a Planter Family of the Old and New South," *Journal of Southern History*, VI (August, 1940), 347-367.
——, "Magnolia Plantation, 1852-1862; a Decade of a Louisiana Sugar Estate," *Mississippi Valley Historical Review*, XXV (September, 1938), 197-210.
Whittington, G. P. (ed.), "Concerning the Loyalty of Slaves in Louisiana in 1863," *Louisiana Historical Quarterly*, XIV (October, 1931), 487-502.
——, "Rapides Parish Louisiana; a History," *Louisiana Historical Quarterly*, XVIII (January, 1935), 5-39.

UNPUBLISHED THESES

Lathrop, Barnes F., "The Pugh Plantations, 1860-1865; a Study of Life in Lower Louisiana," Ph.D. Dissertation, University of Texas, Austin, 1945.
Postell, Paul E., "John Hampden Randolph, a Southern Planter," M.A. Thesis, Louisiana State University, Baton Rouge, 1936.

INDEX

Abbott, John S. C.: read by plantation girl, 134
Adams, Henry, 5
Aichette, 46
Aime, Valcour, 4, 30
Alexandria, Louisiana: capture of, 57; burned by Federals, 65; rum stored in, 87; mentioned, 47, 64, 95
Algiers, Louisiana, 99
Allen, Henry W., 65
Amusements. *See* Social life
Arkansas: engages Federal gunboat, 124; mentioned, 131
Arlington Plantation: and celebration of secession, 22; abandonment of, 53-55; shelled by Federals, 61; and war refugees, 63-64
Ashland Plantation, 67, 70, 73
Atchafalaya River, 1, 42, 58

Baltimore, Maryland, 118
Banks, Mrs. Nathaniel P., 109
Banks, Nathaniel P.: campaigns of, in Louisiana, 55, 57-58; and destruction of plantation property, 66, 69; alters sequestration policy, 73; orders seed cane saved, 84; labor system of, 104-114, *passim*; proclaims slave laws inoperative, 112; replaced by General Stephen A. Hurlbut, 114n; treatment of plantation women, 122; mentioned, 56, 61, 65, 97, 104, 115, 122, 132
Banks, New Orleans: ruined by war, 87-88
Barrow, Bennet H., 7
Barrow, William, 7
Baton Rouge, Louisiana: battle of, 61; mentioned, 53, 55, 63, 66, 67, 68, 71, 76, 86, 93, 94, 107, 124, 131, 135
Bayou Boeuf, 58
Bayou Cypre Mort, 77, 82, 109
Bayou Goula Guards, 24, 25
Bayou Lafourche: course of, 1; area invaded by Federals, 50-53, 57; area retaken by Confederates, 57-58; mentioned, 19, 42, 44, 49, 50, 51, 58, 60, 66, 79, 80, 81, 83, 94, 97, 98, 100, 117
Bayou Sara, Louisiana, 71
Bayou Teche: course of, 1; area invaded by Federals, 55; scene of combat, 58-60; mentioned, 15, 42, 45, 57, 65, 67, 68, 71, 79, 82, 95, 96, 100, 112, 117, 125, 133
Bayou Vermilion, 1, 68
Bayside Plantation, 17, 29, 132
Beaumont, Texas, 45
Becnel, Lezin, 26, 36-37
Bell, John, 20
Belle Chasse Plantation, 73
Benjamin, Judah P.: plantation confiscated, 73; mentioned, 4, 32
Berwick Bay, 59, 95
Bethell, P. C., 34-35, 59
Blockade, Federal: establishment of, 31; effects of, 42-47
Boatner Plantation, 37, 40
Boeuf, Bayou. *See* Bayou Boeuf
Bond, J. B.: abandons plantation, 49; mentioned, 65
Bonnie Blue Flag, 135
Booth, John Wilkes, 127
Boudreau, Captain, 46
Brashear City, Louisiana, 58
Breckinridge, John C., 19
Bringier, M. S., 40
Bureau of free labor, 111
Bureau of Refugees, Freedmen, and Abandoned Lands. *See* Freedmen's Bureau
Burnside, John, 3, 31, 40
Butler, Benjamin F.: invades cane country, 48-52; sequesters plantation property, 72-73; replaced by General Nathaniel P. Banks, 73; inaugurates system of free labor, 101-103; relieved of command of Department of the Gulf, 104; hatred of plantation inhabitants for, 120-121; mentioned, 75, 97, 111, 122

144

INDEX

Cable, George Washington, 136
Camden, Arkansas, 45
Campaign Sewing Society, 38
Camp Crow, 64
Camp Parapet, 93
Cane country: description of, 1-9; invasion of, 48-49, 57-58; abandonment of, 49-56; destruction in, 65-67, 73-74; losses of, 74n, 137n
Chapman, Ewing, 80-81
Charleston Democratic convention, 19, 23
Charleston, South Carolina, 7
Chesnut, Mrs. Mary Boykin, 131
Clothing: shortage of, 85
Coast: definition of, 2; wartime desolation of, 55
Cobb, Howell, 32
Commission merchants: provide credit for planters, 27; ruined by war, 87-88
Confederates: and plantation social life, 37, 131-133; counterattack in cane country, 57-58; seize plantation property, 70-71; punish Negroes, 98
Confederate States Congress, 80
Confiscation, 72-73
Conrad, Charles, 125
Conscription: in the Confederacy, 80; of Negroes, 108-109
Constitutions, Louisiana: of 1864, 112; of 1852, 119
Conway, Thomas W., 111
Cooperationists: among sugar planters, 21-22; attempt to delay secession, 22
Corinth, Mississippi, 117
Cottage Plantation, The, 61
Cotton: engages Federal gunboats, 58-59
Cotton: growth of, replaced by sugar, 3; traded for sugar and molasses, 44-45; failure of, in cane country, 78-80
Credit: dependence of sugar planters on, 27; lack of, 87-88
Creoles: as sugar planters, 3; religion of, 6; and the war, 122
Crops: wartime diversification of, 78-80
Cypre Mort, Bayou. *See* Bayou Cypre Mort

Davis, Jefferson: sugar planters' faith in, 24; mentioned, 37, 88, 108, 117
de Boré, Jean Etienne, 2
De Forest, John W., 49n
Democratic Party: sugar planters join in 1850's, 19; convention of 1860, 19 and n
Department of the Gulf, 104, 110, 114n
Destruction: in cane country, 65-67, 73-74
Diamond, Henry, 125
Diana, 9
Disease: on sugar plantations during Civil War, 86
District of Lafourche: creation of, 72-73; property sequestered in, 73
Donaldsonville, Louisiana: bombarded by Federal fleet, 53; mentioned, 50, 58, 60, 62, 68, 71, 72, 79, 83, 88, 118
Douglas, Stephen A.: support of, among sugar planters, 19-20
Dow, Neal, 121
Dumas, Alexandre: read by plantation girl, 134

Election. *See* Presidential election of 1860
Emancipation proclamation: issuance of, 107; reaction of sugar planters to, 107-108; reaction of Negroes to, 107-108; portion of cane country not affected by, 111
Essex, 61, 124
Evangeline romance, 1

False River, 3
Farragut, David G.: invades cane country, 48, 53; bombards Donaldsonville, Louisiana, 53; mentioned, 71
Federals: establish blockade, 31; looting by, 68-70; maintain discipline among Negroes, 88; stationed on sugar plantations, 88-89; and debauch of Negroes, 99-100; relations with plantation inhabitants, 120-122, 135-136
Flanders, Benjamin F., 114
Food: shortage of, 85
Fords Theater, 127
Fort Jackson: opposes Federal invasion, 48; and Negro refugees, 92-93
Fort St. Philip: opposes Federal

invasion, 48; and Negro refugees, 92-93
Fort Sumter, 28, 36
France: rumor of intervention, 118
Franklin, Louisiana, 25, 60, 82
Freedmen's Bureau, 114
Fremantle, A. J., 55-56
Frémont, John C., 111
Friends of Southern Rights and Separate State Secession, 20
Fuller, E. W., 59

Gardner, Franklin, 132
General Orders: Number 91, 72-73; Number 138, 84
Genl. Hodges, 47
Georgia Landing, Louisiana: battle of, 58
Gettysburg, Pennsylvania: battle of, 118
Gillet, Captain, 46
Grand Junction, Tennessee, 43
Grant, U. S., 57
Gros Tete Fencibles, 25
Guerillas: depredations of, 71-72, 118, 124; cut levees, 85

Halpin, P., 78
Hogshead: definition of, 3n
Hollywood Plantation, 80, 108
Home Sentinels, 24
Horse racing: favorite sport of sugar planters, 7; continues early in war, 39-40
Houma, Louisiana, 51, 98, 105, 106, 121
Houmas Plantation, 3
Houston, Texas, 45
Hunter, David, 111
Hurlbut, Stephen A.: replaces General Nathaniel P. Banks, 114n; regulates Negro affairs, 114-115

Iberville Grays, 24
Immigration efforts, 137 and n

Jackson, Mississippi, 58
Jefferson Rangers, 25
Jefferson, Texas, 45, 46, 47
Johnson, Bradish, 69
Johnson, Kitty, 107
Johnston, Joseph E., 58, 117, 122
Jones, Charles, 19n

Keith, John A., 121
Kenner, Duncan: racing enthusiast, 7; candidate for Confederate States Senate, 32; race horses seized, 67; plantation looted, 70; plantation confiscated, 73; mentioned, 40, 88
King Cotton: illusions concerning, 56

Labor: slave system described, 10-18; Irish immigrants, 14; "Cajun" workers, 14; wartime shortage of, 75n; slave system destroyed, 92; wage system inaugurated, 101-103; system of General Nathaniel P. Banks, 104-114, *passim*; initial inadequacies of free labor, 105-116, *passim*; relations with United States Treasury Department, 115; post-war pattern of, 137-138
Lafourche, 44, 49, 50
Lafourche, Bayou. *See* Bayou Lafourche
Lafourche, District of. *See* District of Lafourche
Lawrence, Effingham: urges secession, 20; role in Louisiana secession convention, 21; describes Federal invasion, 48; leases his plantation, 89; describes plight of Negroes, 99; criticizes free labor system, 102-103; rewards laborers, 103; condemns conduct of Northern soldiers, 121
Lee, Robert E., 117, 118
Levees: planters desire Federal maintenance of, 7; require constant repair, 18; deterioration of, 35-36, 84-85, 101
Libraries: destruction of, 51-52
Lincoln, Abraham: blessed by Negroes, 100; given report on free labor, 103; issues emancipation proclamation, 107; damned by Creole planter, 122; death of, 127; praised by sugar planter, 127-128; mentioned, 108, 111
Linwood Plantation: as home for refugees, 63; wartime sugarhouse party on, 130-131; mentioned, 61, 125
Littlejohn, Maggie, 37
Little Sallie, 46
Livestock: seizure of, 51, 75 and n, 76-78; purchase of, 77-78
Longstreet, James, 118

Looting: by Negroes, 51-53; by Federals, 51, 68-70; by Confederates, 70-71
Louis D'or, 46
Louisiana Historical Quarterly: acknowledgment of, 75n
Louisiana purchase: effect of, on sugar industry, 2
Louisville *Journal*, 32
Lovell, Mansfield, 49

McHatton, James: in Charleston Democratic convention, 19 and n; reaction to secession, 23; abandons plantation, 53-55
Machinery, sugar-making: cost of, 3-4, 14; description of, 16-17
Madewood Plantation, 33
Magill, David Weeks, 125
Magnolia Plantation: location of, 23; operations on, 28-29; production, 29, 103; lack of self-sufficiency, 30; effects of blockade on, 43; overseer resigns, 80; leased by owner, 89; behavior of Negroes on, 92-93; free labor on, 109; mentioned, 25, 48, 96, 103, 124
Mansfield, Louisiana: battle of, 57, 65
Market. See Sugar market
Martin, R. C., Jr., 37
Maryland, My Maryland, 135
Medicine: shortage of, 85
Mellen, W. P., 110-111, 114
Melrose Plantation, 37
Memphis, Tennessee, 43
Merrick, Caroline E., 23n
Militia organizations, 24-25
Minor, Duncan, 26
Minor, M. W., 90
Minor, William J.: as horse racer, 7, 39-40; treatment of slaves, 11-12, 40; death of son, 26; attitude on Confederate politics, 32; race horses seized, 67; provisions taken by Federals, 68; provisions taken by Confederates, 70; conserves livestock, 76; cotton crop fails, 79; problems with overseer, 80-81; Unionist sentiments of, 81; saves seed cane, 84; plantation flooded, 84-85; relations with Federals, 88; asked to form partnership, 90; despondency of, 90, 119, 126-128; Confederates hang a laborer of, 98; and free labor, 105-114, *passim*; and conscription of Negroes, 108-109; reaction to death of Abraham Lincoln, 127-128; mentioned, 97
Mississippi River: course of, in cane country, 1; as avenue of Federal invasion, 42, 53; mentioned, 50, 56, 57, 58, 72, 93
Moore, John: in secession convention, 21; purchases supplies, 30; death of nephew, 125
Moore, Thomas O.: purchases supplies, 30; seeks sugar market, 46-47; violence of Negroes on plantation of, 97-98; mentioned, 70, 77
Mooreland Plantation, 98
Morgan City, Louisiana, 58n
Moss, Spanish: uses of, 105n
Mouton, Alexander: and Charleston Democratic convention, 19; as president of Louisiana secession convention, 21-22

Napoleonville, Louisiana, 135
Natchez, 44
Natchez, Mississippi, 7, 46
Negroes: number of, in cane country, 10; discipline of, 11; religion of, 11-12; treatment of, 11-15, *passim*; amusements of, 15; whites' fear of, 32-36; reaction to Federal invasion, 48-49; looting by, 51-53; disobedience of, 54; taken to Texas, 55-56; destroy property, 66; leave plantations, 76, 92-99; refuse to work, 88; behavior toward whites, 96-98; and jubilee of freedom, 98-100; debauch of, 99-100; and religious freedom, 100; as wage laborers, 102-114, *passim*; reaction to emancipation proclamation, 107-108; under United States Treasury Department, 110; legally free in Louisiana, 112; accused of malingering, 112-113, 114n; disappointment of, 115; conduct condemned by planter, 121; temporary unreliability of, 137; praised by planters, 137-138
New Iberia, Louisiana, 76, 121
New Orleans, Louisiana: port of cane country, 2, 5; entertainment center,

7-9; capture of, 49; and Negro refugees, 92-96, *passim*; and rumors of foreign intervention, 118; psychological effects of capture, 119; mentioned, 45, 47, 58, 72, 73, 76, 77, 81, 84, 89, 99, 101, 106, 108, 109, 117, 120, 121, 122
New Orleans *Bee*, 106
New Orleans *Daily Crescent*, 32
New Orleans *Daily Picayune*: describes desolation of cane country, 56; condemns guerillas, 72; mentioned, 49
New Orleans *Daily True Delta*: and secession of Louisiana, 22; describes seizure of livestock, 67; condemns guerillas, 72; comments on cane and cotton crops, 79-80; analyzes plantation ills, 88n; describes flight of Negroes, 93, 95-96
New Orleans *Price-Current*: summarizes plantation losses, 73-74
New York *Tribune*, 72
Nineteenth Corps, 67
Nordhoff, Charles, 137-138

Oaklands Plantation, 102, 109
Oath of allegiance, 73, 75
Old River, 1
Opelousas, Louisiana: activities of guerillas near, 71, 124; mentioned 78, 132
Opelousas *Courier*, 69
Opelousas Railroad (New Orleans, Opelousas and Great Western), 72
Ouachita River, 45
Overseers: duties of, 11, 13; an overseer's prayer, 23-24; shortage of, 31; and strained relations with employers, 80-81; difficulties in hiring of, 81-82

Page, Nathaniel, 72
Palfrey, Mrs. William T., 123
Palfrey, William T.: supports Confederacy, 25; purchases supplies, 30; indignant over cruelty to Negro, 34-35; fasts and prays for Confederacy, 38; gives slaves holidays, 40; barters for supplies, 46; describes battle on his plantation, 58-60; sells sugar-making machinery, 59; is host to General Richard Taylor, 61; plantation is Confederate camp site, 61-62; death of son, 62, 125; accuses Confederates of looting, 70-71; recovers livestock, 76; borrows mules, 77; problems with overseers, 80; friction with Federals, 81; has typhoid fever, 86; describes flight of Negroes, 95; sends family from plantation, 123; bitterness toward Confederate officer, 125; despondency of, 127
Partisans. *See* Guerillas
Partnerships: formed between planters and entrepreneurs, 89-90
Patrols: re-establishment of, 33-36; laws concerning, 92
Pelican Battery, 59
Perkins, Kitty, 107
Phelps, J. W., 96-97
Plantation ideal: as creative force, 4-5; decline of, 139
Plantation supplies: shortage of, 85-86
Plantation women: role of plantation mistress, 5-6; raise money for Confederacy, 38-39; make Confederate uniforms, 39; witness combat, 60-61; effect on, of war shortages, 85-86; taunt Federals, 121; manage plantations, 122; religious faith of, 123; carry arms, 123; patriotism of, 123; hysteria among, 124; exposed to hazards, 124; lust for Northern blood, 124-125; entertain Confederate soldier, 125; fraternize with Northern soldiers, 135
Plaquemine, Louisiana, 68, 87, 135
Pleasant Hill, Louisiana: battle of, 57, 65
Pointe Celeste Plantation, 102-103, 109
Police juries: appropriate money for volunteer regiments, 25; re-establish patrols, 33-34
Polignac, Charles, 133
Politics: of sugar planters, 7; anxiety of planters concerning, 27; conservative Unionist movement, 119
Polk, Leonidas: insists that slaves be Episcopalians, 11; mentioned, 4
Porter, David D., 48
Port Hudson, Louisiana: siege of, 57-58; visited by plantation families,

133; mentioned, 55, 62, 68, 70, 74, 118, 121, 122, 125, 129, 132, 134
Presidential election of 1860, 19-20
Preston, Texas, 46
Provost marshals: irritate sugar planters, 81-82; assist sugar planters, 88-89
Pugh, A. Franklin: applauds secession, 20-23, *passim*; attends sale of plantation, 27; and local security, 33-34; social life of, 37-40, *passim*; failure of cotton crop, 79-80; smokes last cigar, 85; despondency of, 126; entertains Federals, 135; mentioned, 31, 37
Pugh, David, 33, 97

Quinine: rising price of, 85

Railroads: congestion of, 43
Randolph, John Hampden: subscribes to defense loan, 25; donates money to volunteers, 25; death of son, 125
Ratoons: definition of, 28n
Red River: course of, in cane country, 1; campaigns in area of, 55-56, 57; destruction in area of, 65-66; Negroes leave plantations, 95; violence of Negroes on plantations, 97-98; mentioned, 45, 50, 57, 69
Religion: of sugar planters, 6-7; of Negro slaves, 11-12; as form of social expression, 37-38; engaged in, by liberated Negroes, 100
Remington, Major, 62
Richmond, Virginia, 117
Rillieux invention, 17
Rodrigue, Florian, 33
Rost plantation, 110
Rum: manufacture of, 87
Russell, William Howard: describes plantation life, 4-5; comments on slavery, 12; finds planters' morale high, 24; warns of naval blockade, 30-31; mentioned, 40, 42

St. Martinville, Louisiana, 59
Salt. *See* Plantation supplies
Sarah Plantation, 109
Secession: attitude of sugar planters toward, 20; election of convention delegates, 21; role of sugar planters in, 21-22; of Louisiana, 22
Seed cane: shortage of, 84
Self-sufficiency of sugar plantations: efforts made to attain, 18, 20
Sequestration commission, 73, 104
Seward, William H., 128
Shadows Plantation, The, 61
Sharpsburg, Maryland: battle of, 125
Shenandoah Valley, 57
Shepley, G. F., 109-110
Shiloh, Tennessee: battle of, 117
Shreveport, Louisiana, 46-47
Sinclair, Upton, 87
Slavery: location of slave quarters, 4; description of, 10-18; abolished in Louisiana, 112. *See also* Negroes
Smith, Andrew J., 65-66
Smith, E. Kirby, 47
Social life: description of, before war, 7-9; effects of faraway war, 36-40; continues during invasion and occupation, 129-139
Southdown Plantation, 108
Southern Land Company, 138
Spain: rumor of intervention, 118
Star Plantation, 109
Stephens Guards, 26, 36-37
Sugar: falling price of, 43; exchanged for plantation supplies, 44. *See also* Sugar making; Sugar market; Sugar plantations; Sugar planting
Sugar cane: difficulties of fighting in, 60
Sugarhouses: location of, 4; parties held in, 8, 15, 130-131; description of, 16; looting of, 68-69; decrease in number of, 139
Sugar making: description of, 3, 16-18; filth of, described, 87
Sugar market: slow in 1861, 31; methods of selling, 42; decline of, 43; ruined by blockade, 43-47
Sugar plantations: number of, in 1861-1862, 3; definition of, 3; manorial atmosphere of, 5; as school for slaves, 11; compared with welfare state, 12; depreciation in value of, 27; persistence of routine on, 27, 28-30; abandonment of, 49-56, *passim*; pillage of, 51-56, *passim*, 122; as battlefields, 58-61, 62; outposts located on, 61-62; hospitals impro-

vised on, 62-63; as havens for refugees, 63-64; as a parole camp, 64; destruction on, 65-67; losses suffered by, 73-74 and n, 137; shortage of supplies, 85-86; leased by owners, 88-90; number in operation in 1865, 90, 118; bombardment of, 124; solitude on, 125-126; survive shock of war, 138; post-war value of, 138; shift in ownership of, 138-139; present landmarks of, 139

Sugar planters: men of responsibility, 6; and the tariff, 7; religion of, 7; politics of, 7, 27, 119; attitude toward slavery, 7, 12; social life of, 7-9, 36-40, 129-139; reaction to secession, 22-23; faith in Southern victory, 24; contribute to Confederate cause, 24-25; join Confederate army, 25-26, 36; scoff at blockade, 30-31; replace overseers, 31; abandon plantations, 49-56; hospitality of, 53; accept conqueror's terms, 75; face shortage of livestock, 76-77; lease plantations, 88-90; relations with Federals, 88-89, 120-122; form partnerships, 89-90; retrieve laborers, 93; fear Negro insurrection, 97; prejudice of, against free labor, 115-116; stunned by war, 117; elated by Confederate victories, 117; hear rumors, 117-118; retain belief in necessity of slavery, 119-120; lose sons in battle, 124-125; despondency of, 126-128; host to Confederates, 132-133; visit Port Hudson with families, 133

Sugar planting: description of process, 15-16; difficulties during wartime, 75-91, *passim*, 101-116, *passim*. *See also* Sugar making; Sugar production

Sugar production: in 1861, 27; in 1862, 29-30; in 1863, 103; in 1864, 110; in 1865, 115-116; slowness of post-war recovery, 139

Sultana, 9

Sumter, 71

Supplies. *See* Plantation supplies

Tariff: effect of, on sugar industry, 2; attitude of sugar planters toward, 7, 31-32

Taylor, Hany, 107

Taylor, Richard: condemns the North, 23; and state military organizations, 23; victories over Federals, 57; counterattack in Bayou Lafourche area, 58, 81, 98; guest of sugar planter, 61; plantation stripped by Federals, 66; victory elates planters, 117; dines with plantation family, 132

Teche, Bayou. *See* Bayou Teche

Tennessee River, 117

Texas: as outlet for blockaded sugar, 42-47, *passim*; sugar planters flee to, 49-55, *passim*; Federal prisoners sent to, 121

Thibodaux, Louisiana, 66

Tobacco, 78

Tombola: auction held to raise money for the Confederacy, 38-39

Treasury Department. *See* United States Treasury Department

Twenty-first Indiana Infantry, 65

Unionists: among sugar planters in 1860, 19; meet Federal demands, 75; wartime political activities of, 118-119; entertain Federals, 136

United States Congress, 111

United States Treasury Department, 110

Vandalism. *See* Looting

Varieties Stables, 77-78

Vermilion, Bayou. *See* Bayou Vermilion

Vicksburg, Mississippi, 57-58, 118

Vigilance committee, 33

Waterloo Plantation, 84-85, 90

Weeks, David, 61

Weitzel, Godfrey: invades Bayou Lafourche area, 50, 57; fights in sugar cane, 60; and Negro refugees, 94-95; fears Negro insurrection, 97

Western Sanitary Commission, 110

Whig Party, 19

Whittaker, Overseer, 34-35

Williams, Peter, 107

Women. *See* Plantation women

Woodland Plantation, 102, 109

Yancey, William L., 19

Yeatman, James E., 110

www.ingramcontent.com/pod-product-compliance
Lightning Source LLC
Chambersburg PA
CBHW032258150426
43195CB00008BA/502